TOEIC is a registered trademark of Educational Testing Service (ETS).
This publication is not endorsed or approved by ETS.

Basic TOEIC® for *Science* and *Technology*

サイエンス・テクノロジーで
TOEIC®スコアアップ

Emiko Matsumoto / Kentaro Nishii / Sam Little

EIHŌSHA

はじめに

みなさん、TOEIC 試験についてどう思っていますか？　きっと、「難しい試験」という印象を持っている方が多いのではないでしょうか。でも、大丈夫です。ただただ長い英文を読みこなす試験ではなく、実はパートごとに出題のパターンが決まっています。そのパターンを知り、慣れることで、効果的なストラテジーを身に付けることができます。本書では、そのプロセスを楽しみながら学び、英語学習そのものがもっと身近に感じられるような内容を目指して作りました。

TOEIC® Listening & Reading Test は、多くの企業や大学で英語力を測る重要な試験として位置づけられています。本書は、特に理系分野の学習者に向けて編集された大学用テキストです。初学者から中級者までの幅広いレベルに対応し、基礎力と応用力を効率よく身に付けられる構成となっています。

◆ 本書の特長

本書には、以下のような特長があります。

◎ 理系学生に必要なテーマ

各ユニットでは、理系分野を中心としたテーマを扱っています。たとえば、Unit 1 では「Astronomy / Life Science」、Unit 4 では「Medical Science / Hospital」、Unit12 では「Climatology / Meteorology」など、学生にとって興味深い内容を通じて学習を進めることができます。

◎ 実践的な全 15 ユニット

Unit 1 から Unit14 は、それぞれ 25 問の問題で構成されています。各ユニットで TOEIC の全 Part（Part 1〜 Part 7）を学習することができ、試験形式に慣れると同時にバランスよくスキルを伸ばせます。また、Review では、約 30 問のレビュー問題を通じて総復習を行えます。

◎ テーマに沿った語彙強化

各ユニットの冒頭では、Key Vocabulary として、そのテーマに関連する単語を 6 語ずつ学習できます。これにより、リーディングやリスニングで頻出する語彙を確実に身に付けることができます。

◎ 理系学生に寄り添うキャラクター「コスモ」

各ユニットで登場する「コスモ」が、学習者にアドバイスや励ましの言葉を投げかけ、学習のモチベーションを高めます。

◆ さあ、学びの扉を開けよう！

TOEIC の試験対策はもちろんのこと、本書を通じて「英語を読む」「聞く」という行為そのものを楽しめるようになることを願っています。本書で得た知識とスキルが、皆さんの将来のキャリアに役立つ大きな一歩となることを期待しています。さあ、TOEIC 学習の旅を始めましょう！

2024 年 11 月

著者代表　松本　恵美子

CONTENTS

Unit 1	Astronomy / Life Science		6
Unit 2	Technology / Office Supplies		12
Unit 3	Mathematics / Statistics		18
Unit 4	Medical Science / Hospital		24
Unit 5	Earth Science / Ecology		30
Unit 6	Robots / Mechanics		38
Unit 7	Personnel / Training		44
Unit 8	Shopping / Purchases		51

Contents	テーマ	コラム	Part 1 (写真描写問題) 2問
Unit 1	Astronomy / Life Science	コラム① TOEIC® Listening & Reading Test って何？ 結果はスコアで表示	人物一人の写真
Unit 2	Technology / Office Supplies	コラム② TOEIC® Listening & Reading Test の概要 世界における TOEIC	複数人物の写真
Unit 3	Mathematics / Statistics	コラム③ TOEIC® Listening & Reading Test の概要 試験日程、申し込み方法・受験料	室内の写真
Unit 4	Medical Science / Hospital	コラム④ TOEIC® Listening & Reading Test の概要 受験当日の流れ	室内の写真
Unit 5	Earth Science / Ecology	コラム⑤ Listening Section 攻略法 Listening Section は集中力が鍵	屋外の写真
Unit 6	Robots / Mechanics	コラム⑥ Part 1『写真描写問題』攻略法 基本は主語と動詞	室内の写真
Unit 7	Personnel / Training	コラム⑦ Part 2『応答問題』攻略法 文頭の「疑問詞」を頭に残そう	人物の写真
Unit 8	Shopping / Purchases	コラム⑧ Part 3『会話問題』攻略法 設問は必ず先に呼んでおこう	店舗の写真
Unit 9	Architecture / Housing	コラム⑨ Part 4『説明文問題』攻略法 トークの「種類」は、トーク「前」に確認	屋外の写真
Unit 10	Physiology / Psychiatry	コラム⑩ Reading Section はスピードが命 Part 5 と Part 6 で『時間をかせぐ』、Part 7 で『スコアを稼ぐ』	室内の写真
Unit 11	Aeronautics / Transportation	コラム⑪ Part 5『短文穴埋め問題』攻略法 問題タイプを見極めよう	空港、交通の写真
Unit 12	Climatology / Meteorology	コラム⑫ Part 6『長文穴埋め問題』攻略法 2番目の穴埋めパートもスピード重視で	風景の写真
Unit 13	Employment / Job Hunting	コラム⑬ Part 7『読解問題』攻略法 設問のタイプを意識する	室内の写真
Unit 14	Biology / Zoology	コラム⑭ TOEIC® Listening & Reading Test のスコアの目安は？ TOEFL iBT や IELTS、英検への換算表	動物の写真
Review			

Unit 9   Architecture / Housing ……………………………… 58
Unit 10   Physiology / Psychiatry ……………………………… 64
Unit 11   Aeronautics / Transportation ……………………… 70
Unit 12   Climatology / Meteorology ………………………… 77
Unit 13   Employment / Job Hunting ………………………… 83
Unit 14   Biology / Zoology …………………………………… 90
Review ……………………………………………………………… 97

Part 2 （応答問題）3問	Part 3 3問	Part 4 3問	Part 5 5問	Part 6 4問	Part 7 5問
疑問詞1 (Who, Where, When)	男女2人の会話	アナウンス	動詞の形1	社内回覧	シングルパッセージ
疑問詞2 (Who, Where, When)	男女2人の会話	会議の一部 (図表問題)	動詞の形2	社内回覧	シングルパッセージ
疑問詞3 (What, How, Which)	3ターンの会話	スピーチ	品詞識別1	Eメール	シングルパッセージ
疑問詞4 (Whose, Why, What time…〜)	3人の会話	ラジオ広告	品詞識別2	お知らせ	シングルパッセージ
一般疑問文（Do you 〜等）	図表を含む問題	ガイドツアー (図表問題)	接続詞、 前置詞1	チラシ	ダブルパッセージ
一般疑問文（Did they 〜等）	図表を含む問題	人物紹介	接続詞、 前置詞2	お知らせ	ダブルパッセージ
Be 動詞の疑問文（Is he 〜等）	男女2人の会話	トーク	関係詞	記事	トリプルパッセージ
Be 動詞の疑問文（Was she 〜等）	男女2人の会話	アナウンス (図表問題)	代名詞	Eメール	ダブルパッセージ
提案 / 勧誘する	3ターンの会話	アナウンス	相関語句	記事	シングルパッセージ
依頼 / 許可を求める	3人の会話	留守電メッセージ (図表問題)	比較・最上級	求人広告	シングルパッセージ
否定疑問文（〜じゃないの？）	図表を含む問題	ニュース放送 (図表問題)	品詞識別3	広告	ダブルパッセージ
選択疑問文 (AかBかどちらかを選ぶ)	男女2人の会話	お知らせ	品詞識別4	広告	シングルパッセージ
付加疑問文（〜ですよね？）	3ターンの会話	会議の一部	単語問題1	求人情報	トリプルパッセージ
設問が疑問文の形をとらない場合	図表を含む問題	録音メッセージ	単語問題2	手紙	シングルパッセージ
Unit1〜14まとめの問題					トリプルパッセージ

Unit 1
Astronomy/ Life Science

天文学とは、天体の運動や、宇宙の構造について研究する学問で、ライフサイエンスとは、生命の基本的な仕組みを理解しようとする学問です。

コラム① TOEIC® Listening & Reading Test って何？

▶結果はスコアで表示

　TOEIC（Test of English for International Communication）は、英語によるコミュニケーション能力を測定することを目的としており、合格や不合格といった判定ではなく、スコア形式でテスト結果が表示されます。スコアは、10点から990点の範囲で、5点刻みで与えられます。テストはListening Section（100問、約45分間）とReading Section（100問、75分間）に分かれており、それぞれのセクションでスコアは5点から495点までの範囲で評価されます。試験結果は、英語力のレベルをスコアとして視覚的に示し、受験者の総合的な英語運用能力を反映しています。TOEICのスコアは、世界中の企業や教育機関で英語能力の評価基準として広く使用されており、特にビジネスやアカデミックの場面で重視される指標となっています。

TOEICには1000点や、777点は存在しないんだね。

Key Vocabulary　英語の意味を下記の日本語から選びましょう。

1. planetarium (　　)　2. telescope (　　)　3. exhibition (　　)
4. Neptune (　　)　5. observatory (　　)　6. resident (　　)

A. 展望台　　B. プラネタリウム　　C. 居住者
D. 展示　　　E. 望遠鏡　　　　　　F. 海王星

Listening Section

Part 1 Photographs

英文を聞き、4 つの中から最も適切な描写を選びましょう。

1.
   Ⓐ Ⓑ Ⓒ Ⓓ

2.
   Ⓐ Ⓑ Ⓒ Ⓓ

人物が一人の場合、選択肢の主語は統一されていることが多いよ。

Part 2 Question-Response

設問に対する応答として、最も適切なものを選びましょう。

3. Mark your answer on your answer sheet.　Ⓐ Ⓑ Ⓒ
4. Mark your answer on your answer sheet.　Ⓐ Ⓑ Ⓒ
5. Mark your answer on your answer sheet.　Ⓐ Ⓑ Ⓒ

Part 3 Short Conversation

会話文を聞いて、各設問に対する最も適切な答えを 4 つの選択肢から選びましょう。

6. What is the conversation mainly about?
   (A) The phases of the moon
   (B) The occurrence of solar eclipses
   (C) The difference between the Earth and the sun
   (D) Different types of eye glasses

7. Why does the moon completely cover the sun during a solar eclipse?
   (A) Because it is very close to the Earth
   (B) Because it is the same size as the sun
   (C) Because it is the right size and distance to block the sun
   (D) Because the moon is very far away

8. What should people use to safely watch the event?
   (A) Sunglasses　　　　　　　　(B) A telescope
   (C) Special eclipse glasses　　 (D) Binoculars

Part 4 Short Talk

説明文を聞いて、各設問に対する最も適切な答えを 4 つの選択肢から選びましょう。

9. What is the purpose of the talk?
   (A) To promote the next special exhibition
   (B) To inform visitors of a schedule change
   (C) To introduce the contents of the event
   (D) To explain how to refund a valid ticket

10. According to the speaker, what will most likely happen before 4 p.m.?
    (A) Repair work will be finished.
    (B) The next performance will begin.
    (C) Visitors will be guided to the venue.
    (D) The counter will be closed.

11. What are the listeners asked to do to join the next event?
    (A) Purchase another ticket
    (B) Enter through another gate
    (C) Stay around the counter
    (D) Renew their ticket

Reading Section

Part 5 Incomplete Sentences

空所に入る最も適切な語句の形を選びましょう。

12. The telescope -------- the scientist to observe distant stars clearly.
    (A) enable   (B) enables   (C) enabled   (D) enabling

13. Researchers -------- new data about the planet's atmosphere for the last decade.
    (A) collected   (B) are collecting
    (C) collect   (D) have been collecting

14. The discovery of a new exoplanet will -------- during the conference next week.
    (A) be announced   (B) announce   (C) announced   (D) announcing

15. The observatory was recently ------- with advanced equipment for better data accuracy.

    (A) equipped   (B) equipping   (C) equip   (D) equipment

16. The experiment must be conducted carefully, ------ the results may not be reliable.

    (A) and   (B) but   (C) or   (D) however

Part 6 Text Completion

Questions 17-20 refer to the following memo.

MEMO

To: All the researchers and the staff members
From: Senior Project Managers
Date: January 17
Subject: Award Celebration

On behalf of Luton Institute of Technology, we would like to congratulate our colleagues, Drs. Bremen and Yamada, on receiving such a wonderful award at the nationwide conference in Manchester. Nobody engaging in life science may deny the -------- (17) and creativity of their 10-year-long research.

In contrast to the formal award ceremony -------- (18) at the conference, we have planned a more -------- (19) celebration for them. The party starts at 6 p.m. on January 24 at the cafeteria on the first floor. Anyone who would like to celebrate the young researchers will be welcome for free. -------- (20). If you attend the event, please make sure to e-mail the General Affairs Department by January 20 to confirm how much catered food we need to order.

17. (A) innovation   (B) innovative   (C) innovate   (D) innovated

18. (A) was held   (B) held   (C) will be held   (D) will hold

19. (A) casual   (B) appropriate   (C) expensive   (D) informative

20. (A) Alternatively, please contact the office at extension 303.
    (B) Therefore, a shuttle service among the labs will be suspended.
    (C) Remember, we will be instituting a new research policy soon.
    (D) Additionally, there may be some surprising guests at the party.

Part 7 Single Passage

Questions 21-25 refer to the following e-mail.

Dear Prof. Honobe,

I am sorry for taking so long to respond to your invitation. As an astronomer, I am delighted to hear that the University of Ontario has upgraded its observatory to the world's most advanced level. It would be my great pleasure to attend the grand-reopening as a guest speaker. - [1] -.

Furthermore, I appreciate your generosity in letting my graduate students use your new state-of-the-art telescope at night on the day. - [2] -. However, I will have to leave for the airport in the afternoon, due to a business trip overseas. - [3] -. Therefore, I was wondering if one of your assistants could help my students use the equipment in the evening session.

As for the grand-reopening, I would like to make a suggestion. I once read an article of yours in the online local newspaper where you emphasized how the surroundings of your campus were blessed with nature, which is essential to astronomical observation. So, I think it might be a good chance to invite some local business leaders as well as researchers and town officials to the ceremony. This would foster industry-academia-government collaboration to make more local residents aware of the importance of nature preservation in the town. - [4] -.

Again, thank you very much for inviting me to this wonderful event. I look forward to seeing you and the reborn facility soon.

Sincerely yours,
Karen Mercer

21. Why is Ms. Mercer writing to Prof. Honobe?
    (A) To suggest changing the event schedule
    (B) To invite him to her school event
    (C) To ask him about the number of attendees
    (D) To inform him of her acceptance

22. What is suggested about the ceremony?
    (A) It is supposed to be held in the morning.
    (B) Its venue will be outdoor.
    (C) Some guests will deliver a speech.
    (D) Some students are invited as guests.

23. What is indicated about Ms. Mercer?
    (A) She used to be Prof. Honobe's assitant.
    (B) She teaches at an educational institution.
    (C) She will be taking a vacation abroad.
    (D) She will launch a new project soon.

24. What does Ms. Mercer suggest doing for the event?
    (A) Placing an add in the paper
    (B) Asking local residents for fundraising
    (C) Collaborating with other institutes
    (D) Inviting local business people

25. In which of the positions marked [1], [2], [3], and [4] does the following sentence best belong?
    "I'd definitely like to attend with them."
    (A) [1]   (B) [2]   (C) [3]   (D) [4]

Unit 2
Technology/ Office Supplies

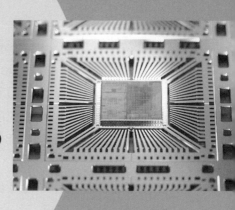

テクノロジーは、科学や工学の知識を使って、日常生活や産業に役立つ技術を生み出すことを指します。オフィスサプライとは、会社や仕事場で使用される文房具や設備のことです。

コラム② TOEIC® Listening & Reading Test の概要

▶世界における TOEIC

　TOEIC は、英語の実践的なコミュニケーション能力を評価するグローバルなテストとして、世界中で広く実施されています。現在、TOEIC は世界 160 カ国以上で実施され、受験者数は年間に数百万人を超えています。日本でも年間約 300 万人が受験しており、その社会的認知度はますます高まっています。

　地域別の平均スコアを比較すると、ヨーロッパの受験者が最も高い得点を示し、それに続くのがアフリカ、北米の受験者です。アジアの受験者はその中でもやや低めで、地域別では 5 位中 4 位にランクされます。さらに、国別の平均スコアランキングでは、日本は最新データで 47 カ国中 39 位と、比較的下位に位置しています。この結果から、日本国内での英語学習の重要性や、ビジネスでのグローバル化が一層求められていることがわかります。英語力を向上させ、国際的な場での競争力を高めるために、TOEIC スコアを伸ばすことが今後の課題と言えるでしょう。

Key Vocabulary　英語の意味を下記の日本語から選びましょう。

1. replenish (　　)　　2. automatic (　　)　　3. suitable (　　)
4. maintenance (　　)　5. extension (　　)　　6. function (　　)

A. 自動の　　B. 機能　　C. 内線
D. 補修　　　E. 補充する　F. 適切な

Listening Section

Part 1 Photographs

英文を聞き、4つの中から最も適切な描写を選びましょう。

1.
   Ⓐ Ⓑ Ⓒ Ⓓ

2.
   Ⓐ Ⓑ Ⓒ Ⓓ

Part 2 Question-Response

設問に対する応答として、最も適切なものを選びましょう。

3. Mark your answer on your answer sheet.   Ⓐ Ⓑ Ⓒ
4. Mark your answer on your answer sheet.   Ⓐ Ⓑ Ⓒ
5. Mark your answer on your answer sheet.   Ⓐ Ⓑ Ⓒ

文頭の疑問詞を頭に残そう。

Part 3 Short Conversation

会話文を聞いて、各設問に対する最も適切な答えを4つの選択肢から選びましょう。

6. What is the main topic of the conversation?
   (A) The installation of new software
   (B) The features of the new photocopier
   (C) Office supply orders
   (D) The layout of the office

会話の主旨は何かな。

7. What is a new feature mentioned by the woman?
   (A) Printing on both sides   (B) Color printing
   (C) Automatic stapling   (D) Scanning directly to email

8. What does the man probably do next?
   (A) Save more office supplies
   (B) Print the project proposal
   (C) Check if the boss received the email
   (D) Arrange a meeting with the project team

Part 4 Short Talk

説明文を聞いて、各設問に対する最も適切な答えを 4 つの選択肢から選びましょう。

[Office Extension Numbers]

Name	Extension
Security Lodge	203
Reception	230
IT Department	302
General Affairs Department	320

9. What is the speaker mainly discussing?
    (A) An updated program
    (B) A system malfunction
    (C) A logistics company
    (D) A software problem

表の情報を分けて、選択肢にない情報に注意して聞こう。

10. What does the speaker recommend avoid doing?
    (A) Contacting the supplier   (B) Using the system
    (C) Downloading software   (D) Scheduling online meetings

11. Look at the graphic. Where is Ms. Ferdinand most likely working?
    (A) Security Lodge   (B) Reception
    (C) IT Department   (D) General Affairs Department

Reading Section

Part 5 Incomplete Sentences

空所に入る最も適切な語句の形を選びましょう。

12. The office manager ------- an email to all staff about the new printer policies yesterday.
    (A) send   (B) sending   (C) sends   (D) sent

13. Before employees ------- access to the company's new intranet system, they must complete a training session.
    (A) gained   (B) gain   (C) gaining   (D) will gain

14. The IT department ------- a new software update every quarter to improve system performance.
    (A) release   (B) releases   (C) released   (D) releasing

15. Once the meeting -------, the team will discuss the new project proposal.
    (A) was concluding   (B) concludes   (C) conclude   (D) concluding

16. The technician ------- the broken printer when he was called to another urgent task.
    (A) repaired   (B) is repairing   (C) was repairing   (D) repairs

Part 6 Text Completion

Questions 17-20 refer to the following memo.

To: All employees at Blue Hills Tech

From: Brian Cheng, International Marketing Section

Date: July 21

Subject: Free evening webinar series

Blue Hills Tech will offer all employees a series of free online seminars for five evenings next week. ------- (17) trends in our industry change so fast, you are highly ------- (18) to attend them. The instructors are all experienced experts from the IT industry and some renowned guest speakers from various fields, ranging from computer science to child education, are supposed to join the webinars.

------- (19). Thus, please be advised to make Zeta, the web conference software, available on your device beforehand. Obviously, it has to be equipped with a camera and a microphone. The timetable will ------- (20) this memo by the end of today. For further information, please contact us at extension 708 or e-mail us at marketing@bluehillstech.com.

---

17. (A) Even if   (B) Considering that   (C) Along with   (D) Regardless of

18. (A) recommended   (B) recommending   (C) recommends
    (D) recommendation

19. (A) You have already been divided into groups.
    (B) You may be too busy to attend the event.
    (C) A sufficient number of computers will be prepared.
    (D) The seminars will be interactive.

20. (A) dispatch   (B) follow   (C) contain   (D) attribute

「文選択問題」は文書の文脈をつかんだ後、4問の最後に解くと解きやすいよ。

Part 7 Single Passage

Questions 21-25 refer to the following advertisement.

'Can anybody solve our urgent computer problems?'
'Of course, We can!'

Having problems with your company's computer system? Are you sure your system is properly protected? Don't you have broken or unused PCs in the storage room?... System Hotline can help your business by addressing these problems quickly and cost-effectively in your local area.

1. System Maintenance
Your company's internal system is always at risk, and regular maintenance is indispensable. Our system engineers can perform thorough checks on your system and are available all year round. Since most system issues happen unexpectedly, including on weekends and holidays, we have engineers on standby at all times.

2. Build an office internal system for your business
With our extensive knowledge, we can design an internal computer system that is perfectly suited to your company, store, or school. First, our experienced staff will visit you to ask about your requirements and assess your workplace. Then, we will present you with proposals and estimated costs within a few days. Whether you are starting a new business or updating your existing system, please feel free to contact us.

3. Provide the best software for you
Today, a wide range of software is available for business use. However, not all software is suitable for every business. We can help you choose the software that best fits your needs. If you're experiencing difficulties with your current software, it may be unsuitable for your business, and our software experts can provide you with effective advice.

4. Solve your device problems

Leaving your office devices unused can incur extra costs over time. To maximize the value of your office supplies, including those currently out of order, we offer repair services for broken hardware such as PCs, smartphones, and tablet computers. If a device is beyond repair, its parts can often be reused in another computer. Embracing the 'reduce, reuse, and recycle' philosophy, we are proud to be an eco-friendly company officially certified by the city.

To check out the video reviews from our present clients, please visit our Web site, www.systemhotline.com.

System Hotline, Ltd.
24 Parkside Avenue, Norfolk, VA 23401

21. Who is the advertisement most likely intended for?
    (A) Parts suppliers   (B) Business owners
    (C) Appliance stores   (D) Internet providers

22. What does PC Hotline, Ltd. do for its customers?
    (A) Improve their Web site   (B) Contact office suppliers
    (C) Reuse their computers   (D) Develop computer systems

23. What is available on the Web site?
    (A) Estimated costs   (B) Some customer reviews
    (C) A list of software   (D) Some blueprint samples

24. The word "indispensable" in paragraph 3, line 2, is closest in meaning to
    (A) essential   (B) expensive   (C) dependable   (D) authorized

25. What is suggested about System Hotline, Ltd.?
    (A) Most of its clients are satisfied with its service.
    (B) Some of its employees work on holidays.
    (C) It provides its software to various companies.
    (D) It is authorized to access the city database.

Unit 3
Mathematics/Statistics

数学も統計も、理系の皆さんにとってなじみが深い分野ですね。専門用語が少し出てきてもチャレンジしてみましょう。

コラム③ TOEIC® Listening & Reading Test の概要

▶試験日程

TOEIC® Listening & Reading Test は、年間で 10 回実施されており、受験者にとって受験機会が豊富です。実施月は、1月、3月、4月、5月、6月、7月、9月、10月、11月、12月です。

▶申し込み方法・受験料

TOEIC の申し込みは、インターネットまたは一部のコンビニ端末を利用して簡単に行うことができます。公式サイトから申し込む場合、ログイン後に希望の試験日を選択し、クレジットカードやコンビニ決済など多様な支払い方法に対応しています。その他、受験料や申し込み方法に関する最新情報は、TOEIC 公式サイトで確認が可能です。現在のところ、TOEIC® Listening & Reading Test はオンラインでは受験できません。受験者は指定された会場に足を運んで受験する必要があります。TOEIC の公式サイトでは試験会場や実施日程が公開されており、受験者は自分の希望する会場を選んで受験する形式となっています。

オンラインではなく、会場で受験するんだね。

Key Vocabulary 英語の意味を下記の日本語から選びましょう。

1. generosity (　　) 2. mock (　　) 3. talent (　　)
4. efficiency (　　) 5. potential (　　) 6. sufficient (　　)

- A. 効率
- B. 十分な
- C. 寛大さ
- D. 才能
- E. 潜在的な
- F. 疑似の

Listening Section

Part 1　Photographs

英文を聞き、4つの中から最も適切な描写を選びましょう。

1. 　　2.

　Ⓐ　Ⓑ　Ⓒ　Ⓓ　　　　　　　　　Ⓐ　Ⓑ　Ⓒ　Ⓓ

Part 2　Question-Response

設問に対する応答として、最も適切なものを選びましょう。

3. Mark your answer on your answer sheet.　　Ⓐ　Ⓑ　Ⓒ
4. Mark your answer on your answer sheet.　　Ⓐ　Ⓑ　Ⓒ
5. Mark your answer on your answer sheet.　　Ⓐ　Ⓑ　Ⓒ

Part 3　Short Conversation

会話文を聞いて、各設問に対する最も適切な答えを4つの選択肢から選びましょう。

6. What was the woman struggling with?
   (A) Memorizing the formula
   (B) Calculating the standard deviation
   (C) Using the new statistical software
   (D) Finding data for the report

7. How does the function on the calculator work?
   (A) Enter the data set and press the 'SD' button
   (B) Input the mean value and press the 'Calculate' button
   (C) Select the data range and press the 'Function' button
   (D) Type in the formula manually and press 'Enter'

8. What did the standard deviation show about the sales figures?
   (A) They were all the same
   (B) They followed a normal distribution
   (C) They were lower than expected
   (D) They varied more than expected

Part 4 Short Talk

説明文を聞いて、各設問に対する最も適切な答えを4つの選択肢から選びましょう。

9. What happened at Marshall's Bookstore last week?
   (A) It received a prize.   (B) It opened a branch.
   (C) It held an event.   (D) It provided the venue.

10. Who is William Gordon?
    (A) A professor   (B) An author
    (C) A business owner   (D) An event organizer

11. What did Ms. Hunt most likely do last year?
    (A) She published the book.
    (B) She obtained a degree.
    (C) She attended a conference.
    (D) She met her former colleague.

Reading Section

Part 5 Incomplete Sentences

空所に入る最も適切な語句を選びましょう。

12. The ------- of the data was essential to draw accurate conclusions.
    (A) organize   (B) organization   (C) organized   (D) organizer

13. The research team ------- analyzed the statistical data to find patterns in the results.
    (A) critical   (B) criticism   (C) critically   (D) criticize

14. The graph ------- the relationship between two variables clearly.
    (A) demonstrating   (B) demonstrated   (C) demonstration
    (D) demonstrates

15. The new algorithm was developed to ------- the efficiency of data processing.
    (A) optimizing   (B) optimization   (C) optimize   (D) optimizes

16. The professor emphasized the importance of statistical ------- in the presentation.

    (A) accuracy   (B) accurate   (C) accurately   (D) accuracies

Part 6 Text Completion

Questions 17-20 refer to the following e-mail.

To:	Brooks Wells <brooks.wells@biz-assist.co.uk>
From:	Emily Nakamura <e.nakamura@greentech.com>
Date:	23 October
Subject:	Re: Invitation

Dear Mr. Wells,

On behalf of Greentech Corporation, I am replying to you to thank you for inviting my company to the Birmingham IT Job Fair this year. Since many skilled IT engineers attend the fair that your company organizes, we are delighted to accept your offer. It was a great shame that we missed ------- the event two years ago due to a scheduling conflict. -------.
(17)
(18)

------- we are pleased to have a booth in this year's fair, I am a little concerned about whether we can connect with the job seekers we are searching for. -------,
(19)
(20)
our marketing department has been seeking individuals with strong statistical skills. We would be grateful for any advice you can provide on how to attract these candidates at the event.

I look forward to hearing from you soon.

Best regards,
Emily Nakamura
Senior director, HR Department, Greentech Corporation

17. (A) attended   (B) attendance   (C) attending   (D) attendant

18. (A) For example, we decided to put a job ad on your Web site.
    (B) We have now adjusted our schedule to ensure our participation.
    (C) However, there was no major improvement to our sales.
    (D) By contrast, the number of our customers was decreased.

19. (A) Despite   (B) In addition   (C) While   (D) Now that

20. (A) Inclusively   (B) Seemingly   (C) Efficiently   (D) Specifically

Part 7 Single Passage

Questions 21-25 refer to the following e-mail.

From:	Jason Andrew <jason.andrew@riversidebs.ac.ie>
To:	Hanna Fischer <hanna.fisher@riversidebs.ac.ie>
Date:	August 31
Subject:	Urgent matters

Dear Hanna,

I am pleased to hear that Riverside Business School has received a number of inquiries about our new online statistics courses. Specifically, I am surprised that we have already received several requests for estimates from companies planning to enroll their employees in some of our courses. That means there is a certain demand for online statistics courses, as we expected. I presume what is behind it is that many companies want to employ workers skilled in handling data in the ever-changing industries.

Considering the number of potential students, their level of math and computer skills will vary. Therefore, at yesterday's staff meeting, we decided to divide the students into three to four groups according to their level. Naturally, having more groups means that we will need more instructors, who are familiar with providing online classes. Could you please begin posting job openings immediately, and, soon after we receive a sufficient number of applications, schedule face-to-face job interviews with the applicants? Additionally, I am considering asking successful applicants to do a mock class both in the classroom and online.

Given the expected increase in demand for our distance learning courses, I think we should hire a few full-time IT technicians rather than outsourcing the IT-related services as we do now. I would like you to discuss this within your department and decide if it is necessary and if so, how many we will need.

If you have any ideas on these matters, please feel free to visit my office when I am in or e-mail me. If necessary, we can have an online meeting when I am away from the office.

Regards,
Jason Andrew, Online Course Director

21. What is the purpose of the e-mail?
    (A) To inform of schedule changes
    (B) To request for some assistance
    (C) To arrange job interviews
    (D) To call a video conference

22. The word "potential" in paragraph 2, line 1, is closest in meaning to?
    (A) prospective   (B) motivated   (C) challenging   (D) promising

23. In which department does Ms. Fischer most likely work?
    (A) A public relations department   (B) An accounting department
    (C) A human resources department   (D) An IT department

24. What does Mr. Andrew suggest doing?
    (A) Introducing new software
    (B) Updating their course contents
    (C) Simplifying their hiring process
    (D) Considering hiring some experts

25. What is implied about Riverside Business School?
    (A) It will increase their budget for new facilities.
    (B) It will have less applications than expected.
    (C) It does not have its own computer-related department.
    (D) It specializes in providing corporate training courses.

Unit 4
Medical Science / Hospital

医学は、人間の体や病気について研究し、治療方法を見つける学問です。病院では、医師や看護師が患者さんの健康を守るために働いています。

コラム④　TOEIC® Listening & Reading Test の概要

▶受験当日の流れ

受験当日は次のような流れで受験が進行します。

（例）
11：45 ～ 12：30	受付
12：35 ～ 13：00	試験の説明、音声テスト
13：00 ～ 15：00	試験開始～試験終了（試験時間は数分長くなる場合もあります。）
15：15	解散

ポイント

試験前には必ず音声テストがあり、リスニングの音声確認が行われます。

試験中は、リスニングとリーディングの 2 セクションを途中で区切ることなく行うため、時間管理が重要です。リスニング後に一息つく時間はないため、集中力を維持しましょう。

当日、咳がひどかったりして、周りに迷惑をかけるのが心配なら、試験前に申し出ておこう。

Key Vocabulary　英語の意味を下記の日本語から選びましょう。

1. medication （　　）
2. simultaneous （　　）
3. recovery （　　）
4. designate （　　）
5. direction （　　）
6. outstanding （　　）

A. 指定の	B. 方向	C. 同時の
D. 目立つ	E. 投薬治療	F. 回復

Listening Section

Part 1 Photographs

英文を聞き、4つの中から最も適切な描写を選びましょう。

1.
   Ⓐ Ⓑ Ⓒ Ⓓ

2.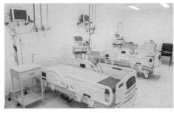
   Ⓐ Ⓑ Ⓒ Ⓓ

Part 2 Question-Response

設問に対する応答として、最も適切なものを選びましょう。

3. Mark your answer on your answer sheet.　　Ⓐ Ⓑ Ⓒ
4. Mark your answer on your answer sheet.　　Ⓐ Ⓑ Ⓒ
5. Mark your answer on your answer sheet.　　Ⓐ Ⓑ Ⓒ

Part 3 Short Conversation

会話文を聞いて、各設問に対する最も適切な答えを4つの選択肢から選びましょう。

6. What is the man's profession?
   (A) Pharmacist
   (B) Nurse
   (C) Doctor
   (D) Medical Technician

選択肢を見ただけで、男性は医療従事者だとわかるね。

7. What issue does the man mention about Mr. Smith's condition?
   (A) High blood pressure   (B) Low blood pressure
   (C) High cholesterol   (D) Low heart rate

8. What side effects did Mr. Smith experience from the medication?
   (A) Dizziness and vomiting
   (B) Headaches and fatigue
   (C) Rash and itching
   (D) Insomnia and anxiety

Part 4 Short Talk

説明文を聞いて、各設問に対する最も適切な答えを 4 つの選択肢から選びましょう。

9. What kind of business is most likely Boots Aid?
   (A) An event organizer   (B) An insurance company
   (C) A pharmacy chain   (D) A travel agency

10. What most likely happened to Boots Aid before October 12?
    (A) It held a fundraiser.
    (B) It opened some branches.
    (C) Its main office was refurbished.
    (D) Its factory was relocated.

11. What are the listeners advised to do until October 21?
    (A) To use a discount coupon   (B) To book a ticket online
    (C) To bring their prescriptions   (D) To apply for membership

Reading Section

Part 5 Incomplete Sentences

空所に入る最も適切な語句を選びましょう。

12. The ------- of the medical equipment is crucial for ensuring patient safety.
    (A) maintains   (B) maintenance   (C) maintaining
    (D) maintained

13. The doctor ------- reviewed the patient's medical history before proceeding with the treatment.
    (A) thorough   (B) thoroughly   (C) thoroughness   (D) though

14. The research study showed a significant ------- in recovery rates among patients.
    (A) reduction   (B) reduce   (C) reduces   (D) reducing

15. The hospital staff must ------- to all procedures to comply with the latest health regulations.

    (A) adhere   (B) adheres   (C) adherence   (D) adhering

16. The nurse provided the patient with a ------- explanation of the post-surgery care process.

    (A) detailed   (B) detailing   (C) details   (D) detail

Part 6 Text Completion

Questions 17-20 refer to the following notice

Dear visitors,

Croydon Hospital will shortly start remodeling the East building. Due to this, we -------(17) our parking rules for visitors at the beginning of June. Since the current car-park is supposed to be used by construction vehicles instead, we will temporarily designate some of the parking lots for our staff members. Any spaces available for visitors will be painted blue, so please use them during the construction. -------(18), you can use any of the local paid car parks such as those of the mall across the street. -------(19). Please be advised to receive a receipt and bring it to the hospital reception, so that you can get -------(20).

17. (A) will change   (B) will be changed
    (C) are changed   (D) have been changing

18. (A) Alternatively   (B) Therefore   (C) Meanwhile   (D) Accordingly

19. (A) You are not allowed to pay at the gate.
    (B) That will obstruct the trucks coming in and out.
    (C) We will cover your parking fee for up to three hours.
    (D) The drivers may be fined in that case.

20. (A) charged   (B) ticketed   (C) reimbursed   (D) deducted

Part 7 — Single Passage

Questions 21-25 refer to the following article.

www.medicalworld.com/news/local

This Month's Feature: 'The Leading Hospital for the Rural Areas'
~ Challenges by Hillside Municipal Hospital ~

By Rebecca Morton

HILLSIDE (September 10) – To celebrate its 70th anniversary of its opening, Hillside Municipal Hospital (HMH) opened a new research center on August 29. The new facility is based on their traditional concept of applying the latest medical research advancements to benefit patients living in remote areas. For those of you interested in visiting, virtual tours are available on the hospital's Web site.

Having been established as the first medical institution in the then Hillside Village in 1955, the small clinic became a nationally renowned hospital. "Along with the development of the village into a city, we have now become a large and leading hospital," says the director of Hillside Municipal Hospital, Colin Ward. "Meanwhile, we've been aiming to achieve top-level medical research for residents of remote areas."

The secretary-general, Louis Young adds, "Since our location is very far from the urban areas, it was very difficult for its residents to access large hospitals for a long time. Naturally, we've been thinking of effective ways to provide our advanced medical practices to patients living in remote areas." In 1970, they renewed the rooftop of our main building into a heliport and started operating air ambulances, becoming the first in the region to do so. With the significant advancement in information technology, they introduced remote surgery in 2015. Recently, they are considering the introduction of Artificial Intelligence into their medical practice.

The HMH is now well-known not only for their medical practice but also for their outstanding contribution to medical science research. "The hospital provides an excellent research environment," one of its senior researchers, Amanda Horton emphasizes. "Our location is blessed with beautiful nature, which provides a calm and relaxing atmosphere. We can even enjoy the hot springs in the mountains behind our site! And I think, after the airport was opened in 2001, we have much better access to international academia. This made it possible for us to invite a larger number of top researchers and medical doctors from both home and overseas."

21. What is the main purpose of the article?
    (A) To recruit new staff members
    (B) To introduce a regional institution
    (C) To announce a new project
    (D) To notify of a refurbishment

22. Who is Ms. Horton?
    (A) A local journalist
    (B) A tour guide
    (C) A city official
    (D) A medical researcher

23. What happened to Hillside Municipal Hospital in 1970?
    (A) It launched a new service.
    (B) It opened some laboratories.
    (C) It was relocated near the airport.
    (D) It hired some IT engineers.

24. What is most likely true about Hillside City?
    (A) It updated the new facility on its Web site.
    (B) It is suffering from a shortage of doctors.
    (C) It was a village when the clinic was opened.
    (D) It has been subsidizing the hospital since 1970.

25. What is suggested about Mr. Young?
    (A) He was brought up in the city.
    (B) He was an assistant of the director.
    (C) He was promoted to senior staff member.
    (D) He was interviewed along with Mr. Ward.

Unit 5
Earth Science / Ecology

地球科学は、地球の構造や気象、地質などを研究する学問です。エコロジー（生態学）は、生物とその環境との関係を探る学問で、環境問題や自然保護にも関連しています。

コラム⑤　Listening Section 攻略法

▶ Listening Section は集中力が鍵

リスニング能力を向上させるには時間と努力が必要です。文章の内容を何度も読み、理解を深め、練習を繰り返し、音声と結びつけて、無意識に理解できるレベルまで持っていくプロセスが大切です。このプロセスを支えるために、一定の時間リスニングに集中できる力が求められます。

TOEIC の Listening Section は、この集中力を鍛えるのに最適です。TOEIC のスコアアップを短期目標としながら、真のリスニング力と集中力を身に付けられるよう、継続的に取り組んでいきましょう。

音声を聞いて、自然に理解できるようになることを当面の目標にしてみよう！

Key Vocabulary　英語の意味を下記の日本語から選びましょう。

1. unfortunately (　　)　2. carbon (　　)　3. precious (　　)
4. conservation (　　)　5. properly (　　)　6. reservation (　　)

> A. 予約　　　　　　B. 炭素　　　　C. 貴重な
> D. 残念なことに　　E. 保全　　　　F. 正式に

Listening Section

Part 1 Photographs

英文を聞き、4つの中から最も適切な描写を選びましょう。

1.
   Ⓐ Ⓑ Ⓒ Ⓓ

2.
   Ⓐ Ⓑ Ⓒ Ⓓ

Part 2 Question-Response

設問に対する応答として、最も適切なものを選びましょう。

3. Mark your answer on your answer sheet.   Ⓐ Ⓑ Ⓒ
4. Mark your answer on your answer sheet.   Ⓐ Ⓑ Ⓒ
5. Mark your answer on your answer sheet.   Ⓐ Ⓑ Ⓒ

Part 3 Short Conversation

会話文を聞いて、各設問に対する最も適切な答えを4つの選択肢から選びましょう。

City	Rainfall (mm)	Attendance
Riverside		40
Hillview	60	80
Greenfield	20	100

6. What is the main topic of the conversation?
   (A) The weather forecast
   (B) Rainfall data and seminar attendance
   (C) Future seminar locations
   (D) Speaker preference and evaluations

7. Which city had the highest rainfall?
   (A) Riverside
   (B) Hillview
   (C) Greenfield
   (D) Riverside and Hillview

8. What does the woman think about the impact of the rainfall on attendance?
   (A) It had no impact.
   (B) The lower rainfall in Greenfield might have encouraged more people to attend.
   (C) It improved the attendance in Riverside.
   (D) It was beneficial for the event.

Part 4　Short Talk

説明文を聞いて、各設問に対する最も適切な答えを4つの選択肢から選びましょう。

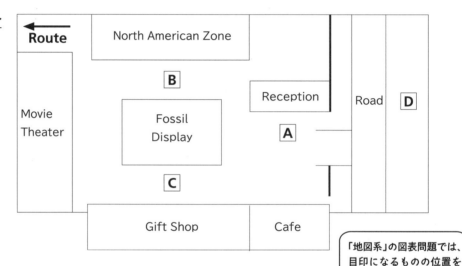

9. Where did the listeners receive the map?
   (A) On the bus
   (B) In the parking lot
   (C) At the reception
   (D) At the tour agency

10. Look at the graphic. Where are the listeners supposed to come after the tour?
    (A) Area A　(B) Area B　(C) Area C　(D) Area D

11. What will the tour conductor do?
    (A) She will check the participants.
    (B) She will distribute brochures.
    (C) She will pay for parking.
    (D) She will take some pictures.

Reading Section

Part 5　Incomplete Sentences

空所に入る最も適切な語句の形を選びましょう。

12. The climate data was analyzed carefully ------- the researchers could predict future weather patterns more accurately.
    (A) but　　(B) although　　(C) so that　　(D) despite

13. The forest conservation project was successful ------- the efforts of the local community.
    (A) because of　　(B) although　　(C) however　　(D) despite

14. The river levels have risen significantly ------- the heavy rainfall over the past week.
    (A) due to　　(B) even though　　(C) unless　　(D) whereas

15. The government passed new environmental regulations ------- some industries opposed them.
    (A) because　　(B) although　　(C) since　　(D) so

16. The project was delayed ------- unforeseen complications, but it was completed successfully in the end.
    (A) because　　(B) due to　　(C) in order to　　(D) whereas

Part 6 Text Completion

Questions 17-20 refer to the following flyer.

Summer Open Seminars for Children Offered
~ Let's observe the nature around your town! ~

Huddersfield University of Science will offer local children, who have an interest in nature, a selection of earth science seminars this summer. --------. For example, the
(17)
marine life seminar will be -------- great help to children looking for a good topic for
(18)
their summer homework. For those with a certain level of computer skills, the meteorology seminar will provide a deeper understanding into climate change issues.

Most of the seminars became full soon after our announcement last year, so we highly recommend submitting your -------- early. -------- your children go to school in
(19)   (20)
Huddersfield Town, they will be given priority to secure their seats.

For further information, please visit our Web site, www.huddersfield.ac.au.

---

17. (A) The fee depends on the seminar they will participate in.
    (B) A variety of interesting seminars will be available.
    (C) Some seminars may be canceled due to low enrollment.
    (D) Each seminar group will consist of five to ten participants.

18. (A) to   (B) at   (C) of   (D) with

19. (A) application   (B) acquisition   (C) attendance
    (D) assistance

20. (A) Since   (B) Whereas   (C) As long as   (D) Owing to

Part 7   Double Passages

Questions 21-25 refer to the following Web page and e-mail.

/www.adamsries.com/

Notice (updated on May 3)

We are pleased to announce that we have received far more visitors and observers than expected after the new facilities were opened. However, we are concerned that such a large number of visitors may damage the precious environment around the institute. Also, welcoming and showing so many visitors around may prevent our staff members from properly carrying out their day-to-day duties effectively.

Considering the situation mentioned above, we now have to limit the number of visitors and observers to just five groups a day. Accordingly, a reservation is required to observe our new facilities from May 5. Please click the button below to make your reservation.

Reserve

Thank you for your cooperation.
The Director of Adams Research Institute of Earth Science

To:	Monica Harwood <monica.harwood@lakelandjr.edu.my>
From:	Linda Emerson <linda.emerson@adamsries.org>
Date:	May 15
Subject:	Your study tour

Dear Ms. Harwood:

Thank you very much for choosing Adams Research Institute of Earth Science (ARIES) for your school trip. Before confirming the reservation you made on May 14, we would like to provide you with some additional information.

First, we understand you would like to visit us at 1 p.m. Unfortunately, another school has also requested a visit at the same time. Considering the total number of visitors from both schools, we will be short-staffed and the facilities may become crowded, which could make the experience less comfortable for your students. To avoid this, we would greatly appreciate it if you could consider rescheduling your visit to the morning on the same day. Would it be possible for us to accommodate your students in the morning instead?

Next, there has been a change to our event schedules. The 'Finding Living Things in the Lake' event, which you would like to attend, is a very popular event among students. However, since the staff members in charge of it will be all busy preparing for the conference for next week, the event for May 24 will be canceled. If you would like your students to participate in an outdoor event, how about the 'Let's Help with the Rice Planting!' event instead, which may provide your students with a deeper understanding of the rice paddy ecosystem. If you are interested in this alternative, please let us know so we can tailor the event to your needs.

Finally, you have reserved 50 Japanese Bento boxes for lunch. Do any of your students have dietary restrictions? If so, we can provide special meals, such as vegetarian or vegan options. Also, we have a beautiful river that runs behind the cafeteria. Although the weather on the day is unpredictable, we would recommend having lunch outdoors.

If you find the above interesting, please log-in to our Web site no later than May 20 and update your booking under the 'Our study tour' tab. Should you have any further inquiries, please do not hesitate to contact us.

Best regards,
Linda Emerson
General Affairs Section
Adams Research Institute of Earth Science (ARIES)

21. What is the main purpose of the Web page?
    (A) To request for cooperation   (B) To make some suggestions
    (C) To promote the institution   (D) To introduce the latest studies

22. Who most likely is Ms. Harwood?
    (A) A travel agent   (B) A research assistant
    (C) A school teacher   (D) An event organizer

23. When is the tour supposed to be held?
    (A) May 14   (B) May 15   (C) May 20   (D) May 24

24. The word "tailor" in paragraph 3, line 9 in the e-mail, is closest in meaning to?
    (A) accommodate   (B) discount   (C) charge   (D) exempt

25. What is suggested about the ARIES?
    (A) It invited visitors to attend free of charge before May 3.
    (B) It opened its new facilities after May 5.
    (C) It allocates a personal account to each booking.
    (D) It hires some staff members specializing in tour operations.

Unit 6
Robots / Mechanics

ロボット工学は、機械やコンピュータを使って、人間の動きを模倣する機械、つまりロボットを作り出す学問です。メカニクス（力学）は、物体の運動や力の関係を理解する学問で、エンジニアリングの基礎となる重要な分野です。どちらも理系の皆さんにとって、とても実践的で面白いテーマですね。

コラム⑥　Part 1『写真描写問題』攻略法

▶基本は主語と動詞

　Part 1 は、1 枚の写真を見ながら、その写真について最も適切な描写を選ぶ問題です。攻略のポイントは、まず全体を把握すること。写真全体の構図や中心にある人物や物を素早く理解しましょう。その後、ディテールを確認し、選択肢に対する準備をします。

　人物が一人だけ写っている写真または、**一人の人物にフォーカス**を当てている場合は、主語は全て同じ語句なので、主語（例：a man, a woman, people）とその動作（例：sitting, holding, standing）が正確に合っているか確認しましょう。**複数人物**が写真に写っていて、それぞれの行動が共通していない場合は、周辺の物に関する表現が正解になることが多いでしょう。**風景、室内の写真**では、建物、家具、車、植物などの位置関係、並び方を説明している問題や、物の状況を説明する問題があります。

写真描写問題で、写真にないものが音声にでてきたら、間違いだね。

Key Vocabulary　英語の意味を下記の日本語から選びましょう。

1. extension （　　）
2. competition （　　）
3. accountant （　　）
4. contribute （　　）
5. tuition （　　）
6. allocate （　　）

A. 授業料　　B. 割り当てる　　C. 競争
D. 貢献する　　E. 延長　　F. 会計士

Listening Section

Part 1　Photographs

英文を聞き、4 つの中から最も適切な描写を選びましょう。

1.
   Ⓐ Ⓑ Ⓒ Ⓓ

2.
   Ⓐ Ⓑ Ⓒ Ⓓ

登場人物の行動と写真が一致しているか確認しながら聞こう。

Part 2　Question-Response

設問に対する応答として、最も適切なものを選びましょう。

3. Mark your answer on your answer sheet.　　Ⓐ Ⓑ Ⓒ
4. Mark your answer on your answer sheet.　　Ⓐ Ⓑ Ⓒ
5. Mark your answer on your answer sheet.　　Ⓐ Ⓑ Ⓒ

Part 3　Short Conversation

図表に関する会話文を聞いて、各設問に対する最も適切な答えを 4 つの選択肢から選びましょう。

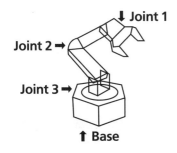

Part	Description
Joint 1	Allows side to side movement
Joint 2	Allows up and down movement
Joint 3	Allows rotation of the arm
Base	Allows the entire arm to rotate

6. What are the people's professions most likely to be?

   (A) Engineers　　(B) Physicians　　(C) Teachers　　(D) Accountants

7. What does the rotating base allow the new robotic arm to do?

   (A) Instructions become user-friendly
   (B) Reach more angles and work faster
   (C) Utilize AI capabilities
   (D) Have a compact design

8. What does the woman think about the impact of the new robotic arm on production?
   (A) It will improve safety.
   (B) It will enhance employee satisfaction.
   (C) It will be more aesthetically pleasing.
   (D) It will improve productivity.

Part 4 Short Talk

説明文を聞いて、各設問に対する最も適切な答えを4つの選択肢から選びましょう。

9. Where does the speaker most likely work?
   (A) At a research center   (B) At an award foundation
   (C) At a publishing company   (D) At a construction company

10. According to the speaker, what happened to the guest in 2008?
    (A) He obtained a degree.   (B) He started new research.
    (C) He won a prize.   (D) He published a book.

11. What does the speaker imply when she says, "rather than go into further detail here"?
    (A) The people do not have much interest in the details.
    (B) The people are already well aware of the details.
    (C) The details are written in a brochure.
    (D) The guest will mention the details later.

このセリフの周辺に答えのヒントがあるよ。

Reading Section

Part 5 Incomplete Sentences

空所に入る最も適切な語句を選びましょう。

12. The team implemented the new algorithm ------- they could enhance the robot's decision-making process.
    (A) since   (B) for   (C) because   (D) so that

13. ------- the system upgrade, the machinery operates with greater efficiency.
    (A) Because   (B) Despite   (C) Although   (D) Due to

14. The project was delayed ------- the engineers encountered unexpected technical issues.
    (A) but   (B) and   (C) because   (D) so

15. The company invested in new technology ------- improve product quality and reduce costs.
    (A) and   (B) for   (C) so   (D) to

16. The team continued testing the prototype ------- it met all safety standards.
    (A) after   (B) until   (C) but   (D) although

Part 6 Text Completion

Questions 17-20 refer to the following notice.

Brentford City Annual Robot Competition

Brentford Municipal Museum is pleased to announce that the 17th City Robot Competition will be held on January 31 as scheduled. Having had our budget reduced due to unexpected repair works on the main building, we launched a crowdfunding campaign for the first time. --------(17). We express our deepest gratitude to the fundraisers. Without their generous support, we --------(18) the competition this year.

Every citizen is eligible to participate in the individual matches, --------(19) old they are. Meanwhile, the team competition will be divided into three categories: high schools, universities and companies. The --------(20) of the application process are now available on the Web site. We look forward to seeing the fruits of your innovative technologies.

---

17. (A) Accordingly, there will be fewer sponsors this year.
    (B) Therefore, we had to reduce the entry fee.
    (C) Obviously, we cannot expect so many participants.
    (D) Fortunately, it resulted in a huge success.

18. (A) could not be held   (B) could not hold
    (C) cannot have held   (D) cannot be held

Unit 6 Robots / Mechanics

19. (A) rather   (B) however   (C) when   (D) whether

20. (A) detailing   (B) details   (C) detailed   (D) detail

Part 7 Double Passages

Questions 21-25 refer to the following advertisement and online form.

Exeter Technical College Opening New Extension Courses
"Let's create your original video game and robot!"

Aren't you interested in developing your own original video games? Don't you want to operate a robot you made yourself? If so, Exeter Technical College is for you. We will be opening new extension courses in our Newport Campus at the beginning of March. Our recently remodeled labs have state-of-the-art equipment and some of them are twice as large as the lab at our main campus.

There will be three categories of courses available by our fabulous experts in robotics, mechanics and computer engineering. Each course will offer three different classes based on skill levels and students will be allocated according to their preferences and computer programming skills.

All you need to do to enroll is write a short program, fill out the application form below and send us both through our Web site. Then, we will decide which course will be best for you.

Once your course is decided, we will e-mail you further information about tuition fees, payment methods and timetables. We look forward to your application.

Name:	Kent Martinez	
Age:	61	
Address:	241 Upper Moore Road, Newport	
Zip Code:	95708 - 0307	
Phone number:	(Home) 555 - 0117	(Mobile) 0883 - 02211
E-mail address:	kentmartinez@firstline.com	
Preferred Category:	Robotics	
Comments: I belonged to a computer club when I was a college student and participated in some programming competitions at that time. However, I guess the current computer languages are far more advanced than those we used. Recently, my grandson asked me if I could make an animal robot for him, which motivated me to create one. Please find attached the game program I wrote a few years ago.		
(sent on February 20)		

21. What is true about Exeter Technical College?
    (A) It has opened some new courses.
    (B) It has updated its facilities.
    (C) It has been recently relocated.
    (D) It has a small number of students.

22. What information is NOT required on the form?
    (A) Postal code
    (B) Current address
    (C) Favorite programming language
    (D) Mobile phone number

23. What are the applicants asked to do?
    (A) Attach a copy of their photo ID
    (B) Create a sample program
    (C) Choose their preferred class
    (D) Make a deposit for the tuition

24. What will Exeter Technical College most likely do for Mr. Martinez next?
    (A) Decide his class
    (B) Contact its instructors
    (C) Send him an invoice
    (D) Sign him up for the contest

25. What is indicated about Mr. Martinez?
    (A) He has never entered into a contest.
    (B) He has a career as a professional programmer.
    (C) He often writes game programs for his grandson.
    (D) He lives in the same town as the college.

2つの文章の関係を考えてから、ヒントはどこにあるのか、一カ所だけにあるのか、分散された複数の情報を統合して解くべきなのか、などを考えよう。

Unit 7
Personnel/Training

人事は、会社や組織の中で人材の採用、育成、評価を行う分野です。トレーニングは、特定のスキルを向上させるための学習や練習を指します。どちらも企業にとって非常に重要な要素であり、効果的な人材育成が企業の成長につながります。

コラム⑦　Part 2『応答問題』攻略法

▶文頭の「疑問詞」を頭に残そう

　Part 2 は、設問を聞いた後、その応答として最も適切な選択肢を選ぶ問題です。Part 2 のみ、選択肢は4つではなく3つです。写真を見たり、設問を読んだりといった視覚的情報を使わずに、リスニング力のみが試されるパートであり、瞬時に意味や状況を把握することが重要です。

　まず、文頭の語句の聞き取りが非常に大切です。例えば、**疑問詞で始まる質問の場合、その疑問詞を頭に残しておく**ことがポイントです。選択肢 A、B、C を全て聞き、正解を導く際にはその疑問詞を意識しましょう。また、疑問詞以外の形式の質問でも、設問が投げかけられた場面や話者の意図を想像しながら答えることが求められます。

　さらに重要なのは**「会話の流れ」を意識**することです。質問文の内容を正しく把握し、会話の展開に応じた適切な応答を選ぶように心がけましょう。これにより、リスニングセクションで高得点を狙うことが可能になります。

例えば、Who で始まったら、「Who, 誰、だれ、だれ…」と心の中でつぶやきながら、選択肢が流れてくるのを待とう。

Key Vocabulary　英語の意味を下記の日本語から選びましょう。

1. application (　　)
2. emphasize (　　)
3. approval (　　)
4. courtyard (　　)
5. inclement (　　)
6. urgent (　　)

| A. 申し込み | B. 緊急の | C. 承認 |
| D. 強調する | E. 中庭 | F.（天候が）厳しい |

Listening Section

Part 1 Photographs

英文を聞き、4つの中から最も適切な描写を選びましょう。

1.  Ⓐ Ⓑ Ⓒ Ⓓ

2. Ⓐ Ⓑ Ⓒ Ⓓ

Part 2 Question-Response

設問に対する応答として、最も適切なものを選びましょう。

3. Mark your answer on your answer sheet.　Ⓐ Ⓑ Ⓒ
4. Mark your answer on your answer sheet.　Ⓐ Ⓑ Ⓒ
5. Mark your answer on your answer sheet.　Ⓐ Ⓑ Ⓒ

Part 3 Short Conversation

会話文を聞いて、各設問に対する最も適切な答えを4つの選択肢から選びましょう。

6. When does the new training program start?
   (A) Last month
   (B) Last week
   (C) Next week
   (D) Next month

7. What is the purpose of the new training program?
   (A) To introduce new software
   (B) To improve project management and assess hires
   (C) To organize a company event
   (D) To evaluate employee performance

8. What does the man need to do before deciding to attend the training?
   (A) Confirm the training details
   (B) Finish his current project
   (C) Get approval from his manager
   (D) Check his schedule

Part 4 Short Talk

説明文を聞いて、各設問に対する最も適切な答えを4つの選択肢から選びましょう。

9. What is the main purpose of the talk?
   (A) To describe the job
   (B) To explain about the industry
   (C) To recruit employees
   (D) To provide instructions

10. What are the listeners advised NOT to do during the tour?
    (A) Leave the group
    (B) Take a video
    (C) Touch the equipment
    (D) Talk to the researchers

11. What will most likely be provided for the listeners?
    (A) An ID tag
    (B) A smart card
    (C) Some food
    (D) Some documents

Reading Section

Part 5 Incomplete Sentences

空所に入る最も適切な語句の形を選びましょう。

12. The manager selected the candidate ------- had the most experience in project management.
    (A) who   (B) which   (C) whom   (D) whose

13. The training program was designed to address the areas ------- employees needed the most improvement.
    (A) tha   (B) which   (C) where   (D) who

14. The company, ------- headquarters are located in New York, has expanded its operations globally.
    (A) which   (B) where   (C) who   (D) whose

15. The HR team conducted interviews with all applicants ------- resumes highlighted relevant skills.
    (A) that   (B) whom   (C) whose   (D) which

16. The mentor explained the process to the new hires ------- they would understand the company's workflow.

    (A) in order to   (B) so that   (C) because   (D) where

関係詞の問題では、空所の前にあるのは人か、物か、そして空所の後の文の形を見て判断しよう。

Part 6 Text Completion

Questions 17-20 refer to the following article.

CARLOW (10 August) — Limerick Chemical Co., Ltd. announced that it had entered into a cooperation ------- (17) with Carlow University to start their industry-academia collaborative project. Initially, Carlow University will begin providing its online education program in September for all new recruits at Limerick Chemical.

Diana Harris, the Secretary General of Carlow University emphasizes, "A variety of courses, ranging from accounting to languages, ------- (18) live. The latest sound technology enables us to make the recruits feel ------- (19) they were in the classroom! ------- (20). I believe our partnership will surely become a role model for other educational institutions and corporations."

17. (A) agreeable   (B) agree   (C) agreement   (D) agreed

18. (A) will be streamed   (B) to stream
    (C) are streaming   (D) have been streamed

19. (A) similarly   (B) likewise   (C) the same   (D) as if

20. (A) However, the number of computers available is very limited.
    (B) Therefore, the application process has not been fixed yet.
    (C) After that, the list of course contents will be available.
    (D) For their convenience, the courses will also be available on demand.

Part 7 Triple Passages

3つの文章の関係を考えてから、それぞれの設問はどの文章を読めばよいのか、予測を立てて読んでみよう。

Questions 21-25 refer to the following schedule and e-mails.

Schedule for the Summer Internship Orientation
(as of July 10)

9:30 ~	Opening Remarks Austin Grant, Director of the Human Resources Department
9:40 ~	Ice-breaking Session (all the interns)
10:20 ~	Logistics Center Tour Elena Jennings, Center Manager
11:50 ~	Outdoor Lunch (Barbeque party in groups)
13:10 ~	Computer Workshop Greg Richardson, IT Department
14:40 ~	Meeting with the Directors (interns from groups according to their departments)

To:	Human Resources Department <hr-dpt@gr.norton-logistics.com>
From:	Austin Grant <a.grant@norton-logistics.com>
Date:	July 17
Subject:	Tomorrow's Orientation

Dear all,

According to the weather forecast, we will have inclement weather tomorrow morning. Considering the situation, we may have to make some changes to the intern's orientation schedule.

First, transportation delays and cancelations are highly likely, especially early in the morning. Accordingly, it is expected that some of the interns who commute by train or bus probably won't be able to attend the first morning session. Why don't we cancel my opening remarks and the ice-breaking session and delay the starting time of the orientation to 10:30 A.M.? Also, since they will have to walk outdoors in some parts of the logistics center tour, I'll ask the center manager if it can be rescheduled for the afternoon.

Next, I don't think we can enjoy the outdoor lunch party in the garden tomorrow. It is regrettable to cancel it, but what do you all think about having an indoor party in the cafeteria instead? If you agree, I was wondering if any of you could choose a good caterer, which can handle our urgent request, and order catering for 30 people.

Additionally, having suddenly accepted three more interns yesterday, they will need their internal computer accounts in tomorrow's workshop. Someone from the IT Department is supposed to take care of it. Could any of you send them a reminder, please?

Here in Castleton, the rain is getting heavier and the wind is getting stronger.

I hope my flight won't be canceled this evening so that I can get home within today.

Please take care,
Austi

To:	Karen Foster <k.foster@norton-logistics.com>
From:	Greg Richardson <g.richardson@norton-logistics.com>
Date:	July 18
Subject:	Today's Orientation

Good morning, Karen.
I hope you managed to drive to the company safe and sound. The wind was so strong that it took me twice as long as usual to walk from my house to the office.

We in the IT department were informed yesterday evening that the logistics center tour had been switched with the computer workshop. We were supposed to get their internal computer accounts ready in advance but we need their personal details to create their accounts. Therefore, they will use a tentative account in the workshop instead.

Apparently, the weather seems to be improving earlier than forecasted, and it is good to hear that the barbeque party in the courtyard will be held as scheduled. At the same time, it is a shame we will miss the indoor luncheon, because you would have found a good caterer and chosen a wonderful menu. We all know you are familiar with some of the best restaurants in town. Anyway, I will see you later at the party.

Have a good day,
Greg

21. What is the purpose of the first e-mail?
    (A) To suggest some schedule changes
    (B) To confirm the revised plan
    (C) To inform his coworkers of the additional sessions
    (D) To update the participants about the event

22. When will the tour start?
    (A) At 9:40 A.M.
    (B) At 10:20 A.M.
    (C) At 1:10 P.M.
    (D) At 2:40 P.M.

23. What is implied about Ms. Foster?
    (A) She belongs to the same department as Mr. Richardson.
    (B) She reminded Mr. Grant of the schedule.
    (C) She was supposed to place an order for the catering.
    (D) She commutes to the company by train.

24. Which event will be most likely cancelled?
    (A) The Ice-breaking Session
    (B) The Logistics Center Tour
    (C) The Outdoor Lunch
    (D) The Computer Workshop

25. What is NOT implied about Mr. Richardson?
    (A) He walks from his house to work.
    (B) He will meet the interns at lunch.
    (C) He personally contacted Mr. Grant on July 17.
    (D) He belongs to a different department from Ms. Foster.

Unit 8
Shopping/ Purchases

ショッピングは、商品を購入するために店に行ったり、オンラインで注文することを指します。購買は、企業が必要な物資やサービスを仕入れる活動です。どちらも日常生活やビジネスの中で欠かせない行動です。目的や規模が少し異なりますね。

コラム⑧　Part 3『会話問題』攻略法

▶設問は必ず先に読んでおこう

　Part 3 では、男女 2 人または 3 人の会話を聞き、その後に設問が 3 問出されます。各設問に対して 4 つの選択肢があり、適切な回答を選ぶ形式です。男性、女性それぞれの**立場や会話の流れをしっかりと理解**して、正解を選びましょう。

　Part 3 では、リスニング力だけでなく、設問や選択肢を瞬時に読み取る速読力も必要です。会話を正確に聞き取る力に加え、単語力や主語と動詞、目的語の関係を正しく理解する構文力も重要になります。

　また、**音声が流れる前に設問と選択肢を先に読んでおくこと**が効果的です。設問を読むことで、会話文を聞く際にどの情報に注目すべきかが明確になり、ここに集中すれば効率的に得点を獲得できるでしょう。

設問を先読みすると、あらかじめ音声の内容が予測できるんだね。

Key Vocabulary　英語の意味を下記の日本語から選びましょう。

1. branch (　　)
2. affordable (　　)
3. replacement (　　)
4. malfunction (　　)
5. renovation (　　)
6. experiment (　　)

A. 手ごろな　　B. 実験　　C. 支店
D. 改修　　　　E. 交換　　F. 故障

Listening Section

Part 1 Photographs

英文を聞き、4つの中から最も適切な描写を選びましょう。

1.
   Ⓐ Ⓑ Ⓒ Ⓓ

2.
   Ⓐ Ⓑ Ⓒ Ⓓ

Part 2 Question-Response

設問に対する応答として、最も適切なものを選びましょう。

3. Mark your answer on your answer sheet.　　Ⓐ　Ⓑ　Ⓒ
4. Mark your answer on your answer sheet.　　Ⓐ　Ⓑ　Ⓒ
5. Mark your answer on your answer sheet.　　Ⓐ　Ⓑ　Ⓒ

Part 3 Short Conversation

会話文を聞いて、各設問に対する最も適切な答えを4つの選択肢から選びましょう。

6. What are the speakers discussing?
   (A) The purchase of a new microscope
   (B) The location of their lab
   (C) The results of their experiments
   (D) The schedule for their research

7. Why does the woman prefer the Zeiss microscope?
   (A) It has a better registration procedure.
   (B) It has higher resolution and better features.
   (C) It has good user reviews.
   (D) It has sufficient functions.

8. What does the man need to do next?
   (A) Confirm the delivery date　　(B) Test the equipment
   (C) Check the budget　　(D) Place the order

Part 4 Short Talk

説明文を聞いて、各設問に対する最も適切な答えを 4 つの選択肢から選びましょう。

The Special Events at Morrisons Appliance

Venue	Event
1st Floor	"Mobile Carriers Show"
2nd Floor	"Best Computer for You"
3rd Floor	"Home Appliances Fair"
4th Floor	"Latest Game Consoles"

9. What is the announcement mainly about?
   (A) A grand opening   (B) A renovation plan
   (C) Some seasonal sales   (D) Some new products

10. Look at the graphic. Which floor will most likely be renovated?
    (A) 1st Floor   (B) 2nd Floor   (C) 3rd Floor
    (D) 4th Floor

11. What can the listeners do online?
    (A) Apply for membership   (B) Use a promotional code
    (C) Browse for items   (D) Download floor maps

Reading Section

Part 5 Incomplete Sentences

空所に入る最も適切な語句を選びましょう。

12. The customer asked the sales representative if ------- could get a discount on the bulk purchase.
    (A) he   (B) his   (C) himself   (D) their

13. The store offers a loyalty program for ------- who frequently shop there.
    (A) those   (B) it   (C) they   (D) them

14. The manager reminded the staff to check the inventory by ------- before closing the store.
    (A) themselves   (B) them   (C) their   (D) they

15. Customers appreciate the convenience of online shopping because it allows ------- to compare prices easily.
    (A) theirs   (B) them   (C) they   (D) their

16. The company is planning to expand ------- operations to new markets next year.
    (A) it   (B) its   (C) they   (D) theirs

Part 6 Text Completion

Questions 17-20 refer to the following e-mail.

To:	Customer Service <customer@bic-online.com>
From:	Ellie Huffman <ellie.huffman@finglands.net>
Date:	November 3
Subject:	Urgent inquiry

I purchased a stylus pen, the SP37 from your online store a few days ago and the item reached me as scheduled. --------, the stylus pen is not working properly with my touch-screen tablet, the TSC35B. I think the stylus should fit my tablet, but maybe I am wrong. Regardless of whether I purchased the right stylus or not, I will return it to you by express mail tomorrow. I would appreciate it if you could dispatch a -------- immediately.--------.
(17)
(18)   (19)

-------- the above, I have been impressed by the affordable prices you offer and
(20)
the quality of your items. I look forward to buying other home appliances from this shop in the future.

Thank you in advance.

17. (A) Effectively   (B) Regrettably   (C) Specifically   (D) Namely

18. (A) refund   (B) replacement   (C) return   (D) reimbursement

19. (A) I understand that the stylus is normally sold separately.
    (B) I am sure I was eligible to get a full refund.
    (C) I was supposed to receive an invoice from you.
    (D) I need to use it for my presentation next week.

20. (A) Regardless of   (B) According to
    (C) Because of   (D) Just as

Part 7 Double Passages

Questions 21-25 refer to the following e-mails.

To:	Customer Care Team <customercare@first-appliance.com>
From:	Thomas Gilbert <thomas.gilbert@finglands.com>
Date:	September 14
Subject:	My request

I purchased a Canox printer at my local First Appliance shop on September 10. Unfortunately, it often gets jammed and the ink from the printer runs. To have the item exchanged for a new one, I filled out the replacement request form attached to the item and sent both the item and the form to the address shown in the instructions the following day.

Although I followed the exchange policy on your Web site correctly and completed the request process within the required time limit, as of today, I have not received a replacement from you. Since I am supposed to print out invitation cards soon, I need this printer as quickly as possible. Could you please check the status of my request and update me at your earliest convenience?

Thank you.
Thomas

2つの e-mail はどのような関係にあるんだろうね。

To:	Thomas Gilbert <thomas.gilbert@finglands.com>
From:	Melissa Hardy <melissa.hardy@first-appliance.co.uk>
Date:	September 15
Subject:	Re: My request

Dear Mr. Gilbert,

Thank you very much for shopping at First Appliance. I am writing in response to your e-mail that we received yesterday regarding your request. We immediately checked our online database and examined the purchase records from the Hastings branch. Consequently, it turned out that your request is pending. The printer you sent us has been carefully examined in our repair center in Crewe. Our repair team also contacted Canox Co., Ltd. to ask for their opinion.

They concluded that the malfunction you experienced could have been avoided if you had used genuine Canox ink. According to their report, the ink that remained in the printer was a compatible product. As stated in the instruction manual, using compatible products other than Canox may damage the item.

Although you made no mistakes in the exchange process, we are afraid to inform you that repair and shipment costs will be incurred in this case. However, as a token of our gratitude for your continued patronage, we will cover all of your additional shipping fees that this may cause you. When the repair cost is estimated, we will inform you immediately.

Additionally, I understand from your e-mail that you urgently need to print invitation cards. Why not take advantage of our free printing service for Canox printer customers? It will only take a couple of days to print up to 200 copies, which should help you meet your deadline.

Kind regards,
Melissa Hardy
Customer Care Team Representative, First Appliance Co., Ltd.

21. According to the first e-mail, what is the problem?
    (A) A shipment has not arrived yet.
    (B) A manual is not enclosed.
    (C) An item is malfunctioning.
    (D) A part does not fit the product.

22. What did Mr. Gilbert NOT do before September 14?
    (A) Completed a form   (B) Shipped an item
    (C) Placed another order   (D) Checked the instructions

23. According to the second e-mail, what will Mr. Gilbert receive?
    (A) A discount coupon   (B) Some genuine accessories
    (C) A replacement   (D) Free shipment services

24. The word "examined" in paragraph 1, line 3, in the second e-mail, is closest in meaning to?
    (A) inspected   (B) passed   (C) collected   (D) preserved

25. What is implied about Mr. Gilbert?
    (A) He used a risky product in his appliance.
    (B) He missed updating his contact details online.
    (C) He has recently moved into Hastings.
    (D) He lives near the Crewe repair center.

Unit 9
Architecture/ Housing

建築は、建物や構造物を設計・建設する技術やアートのことです。住宅は、私たちが生活するための住まいを指します。建築の技術が進歩すると、より快適で安全な住環境が実現します。

コラム⑨ Part 4『説明文問題』攻略法

▶トークの「種類」は、トーク「前」に確認

「Part 3 と Part 4、どちらが解きやすい？」…皆さんはどちらですか。私の印象では、答えは「真っ二つ」に分かれます。「Part 3 得意派」は、「Part 4 では1人の話し手が一方的に話すので早口に聞こえる」など。一方、「Part 4 得意派」は、「Part 3 では複数の話し手が登場し、会話の展開が予想しづらい」など。

Part 4 で話されるのは**限られた種類のトーク**です。しかも、**トークが流れる前に**そのトークの種類が明言されます。"**Questions 71 through 73 refer to the following トークの種類.**" トーク直前のこのナレーションをしっかり聞くことで、トークの種類が分かるので、内容の予測がしやすくなります。

Key Vocabulary 英語の意味を下記の日本語から選びましょう。

1. committee (　　)　　2. mayor (　　)　　3. aquarium (　　)
4. contractor (　　)　　5. blueprint (　　)　　6. resident (　　)

A. 設計図　　B. 委員会　　C. 水族館
D. 市長　　　E. 居住者　　F. 請負人

Listening Section

Part 1 Photographs

英文を聞き、4つの中から最も適切な描写を選びましょう。

1.
   Ⓐ Ⓑ Ⓒ Ⓓ

2.
   Ⓐ Ⓑ Ⓒ Ⓓ

Part 2 Question-Response

設問に対する応答として、最も適切なものを選びましょう。

3. Mark your answer on your answer sheet.　　Ⓐ Ⓑ Ⓒ
4. Mark your answer on your answer sheet.　　Ⓐ Ⓑ Ⓒ
5. Mark your answer on your answer sheet.　　Ⓐ Ⓑ Ⓒ

Part 3 Short Conversation

会話文を聞いて、各設問に対する最も適切な答えを4つの選択肢から選びましょう。

6. What are the speakers discussing?
   (A) The location of their new office
   (B) The schedule for their current project
   (C) The results of their last meeting
   (D) The design plans for the office renovation

7. What concern does the man have about the new design?
   (A) It will be too expensive.
   (B) It will not have enough space.
   (C) It will take too long to complete.
   (D) It will be too noisy without walls.

8. What is a feature of the new conference rooms?
   (A) Glass decorations
   (B) Scheduling boards
   (C) A modern feeling of space
   (D) Movable walls

設問を見ておけば、「会議室」について出てくる会話だと予測がつくね。

Part 4　Short Talk

説明文を聞いて、各設問に対する最も適切な答えを 4 つの選択肢から選びましょう。

9. Where is the announcement most likely taking place?
   (A) On a walkway
   (B) On a beach
   (C) In the yard
   (D) In the lab

10. According to the speaker, what is the main feature of the new facilities?
    (A) They are more spacious than the old ones.
    (B) They are equipped with advanced technologies.
    (C) They are located along the seashore.
    (D) They are made of natural resources.

11. What does the speaker imply when she says, "the conference hall is available all day"?
    (A) The conference is anticipated to last a long time.
    (B) The hall is ready to accommodate the media.
    (C) The outdoor event can be rescheduled.
    (D) The indoor facilities are hardly used.

Reading Section

Part 5　Incomplete Sentences

空所に入る最も適切な語句の形を選びましょう。

12. The renovation project will include both updating the plumbing ------- installing new electrical wiring.
    (A) and   (B) nor   (C) only   (D) also

13. The design of the new office building is focused on creating spaces that are not only functional ------- stylish.
    (A) and   (B) but also   (C) or   (D) as

14. The architects proposed adding large windows to either maximize natural light ------- reduce energy costs.
    (A) but   (B) and   (C) nor   (D) or

15. No matter how innovative the new design may be, it must ------- all safety regulations.

    (A) meet   (B) to meet   (C) meets   (D) meeting

16. The community decided to focus on sustainable practices rather ------- cutting down trees for new developments.

    (A) than   (B) then   (C) whether   (D) when

Part 6 Text Completion

Questions 17-20 refer to the following article.

Coventry Municipal Library Reopens after Renovation

COVENTRY (21 July) — According to the city hall, the remodeling of Coventry Municipal Library has been successfully completed, and it will reopen on July 25.

The renovation was initially scheduled for completion in June. -------- (17). Mayor Catherine Lindsey reflected on the process, stating, "When the first plan was announced by the previous mayor, there were a lot of complaints and suggestions from local residents, especially about cutting down so many trees." Subsequently, the details of the plan were -------- (18) reviewed from multiple perspectives with various people, ranging from construction engineers to botanists. About a month -------- (19) schedule, the revised plan -------- (20) by the city council on April 28, and a tender for contractors was placed the following month.

17. (A) However, it was delayed due to several revisions to the plan.
    (B) Therefore, city officials apologized for their misunderstanding.
    (C) A press conference was not held in the renewed building.
    (D) Most local people were concerned about the budget.

18. (A) approximately   (B) thoroughly
    (C) prominently   (D) apparently

19. (A) before   (B) on   (C) behind   (D) as

20. (A) approved (B) will be approved
    (C) was approved (D) is being approved

Part 7 Single Passage

Questions 21-25 refer to the following text-message chain.

Kate Setter (10:12 A.M.)
Hi, everyone. You've heard that our apartment building may need a major renovation this year, haven't you?

Simon Nicholson (10:13 A.M.)
Hi, Kate, thank you for taking good care of our apartments as always. Yes, I've seen the notice.

Jane Rooney (10:14 A.M.)
I heard about it. Is there anything we have to do?

Kate Setter (10:15 A.M.)
Yes, there are some details on the notice board by the entrance.

Jane Rooney (10:16 A.M.)
Sorry, I've not checked it yet. What should we do?

Kate Setter (10:17 A.M.)
Normally, to estimate renovation costs, contractors need to check in advance the conditions of the facilities, including your privately owned areas. That means they will likely come into your apartments. I'll e-mail all of you the details later.

Simon Nicholson (10:18 A.M.)
Kate, do you think the contractors will point out any problems with this building?

Kate Setter (10:19 A.M.)
Unfortunately, I think they will, because I've recently received a lot of complaints about its facilities, such as water leaks, elevator breakdowns and cracks in the walls, from some of the residents.

Jane Rooney (10:20 A.M.)
I'd agree to some renovations, but I am worried about how much they will cost.

Simon Nicholson (10:21 A.M.)
Me too. I guess that the contractors will recommend replacing the sewage pipes and water-proofing the roof at least.

Kate Setter (10:22 A.M.)
Yes, and there could be more than that. Why don't we organize a renovation planning committee to discuss the issues and choose the best contractor for us among them?

62

21. What most likely will the residents receive soon?
    (A) Announcement of a meeting
    (B) Requests for checking their rooms
    (C) Preparation details for an event
    (D) Estimated costs of refurbishment

22. What is the group concerned about?
    (A) Repair cost   (B) Balcony damage
    (C) Water leaks   (D) Elevator malfunctions

23. What is suggested about the upcoming event?
    (A) It may be harder to walk through the entrance.
    (B) It is regularly held in the apartment block.
    (C) Apartments will be inspected.
    (D) A meeting will be called before the event.

24. At 10:14 A.M., what does Ms. Rooney mean when she writes, "Is there anything we have to do?"?
    (A) She has not heard about the committee plans.
    (B) She wants to make sure of the meeting schedule.
    (C) She has not been updated about the apartment project.
    (D) She is surprised at changes in the apartment's policy.

25. What is most likely true about Ms. Setter?
    (A) She is in charge of maintenance works for the apartment.
    (B) She is supposed to chair the new committee.
    (C) She has some knowledge of apartment renovation process.
    (D) She has inspected another property.

Unit 10
Physiology/ Psychiatry

生理学は、私たちの体がどのように機能するかを研究する学問です。精神医学は、心の健康や障害について研究し、治療する分野です。体と心の関係は密接で、健康を保つためにはどちらも大切ですね。

コラム⑩　Reading Section はスピードが命

▶ Part 5 と Part 6 で『時間をかせぐ』、Part 7 で『スコアを稼ぐ』

　TOEIC の Reading Section では、「100 問を 75 分で解く」ことが求められ、受験者の多くが時間不足に悩まされます。では、どのような対策ができるのでしょう。

　対策方法は現時点でのスコアによって異なるでしょうが、共通して言えることは、「**時間さえあれば正解できる問題を全て解ききること**」ではないでしょうか。

　例えば Part 5 と Part 6 を合わせて 20 分程で解けるようになると、Part 7 に使える時間が増えます。すると、今まで Part 7 に「時間不足で手が付けられなかった問題」が多かった受験者は、**より多くの設問を解くだけで**スコア・アップにつながる可能性があります。

TOEIC の Reading は時間との戦いだよ。

Key Vocabulary　英語の意味を下記の日本語から選びましょう。

1. cognitive （　　）　　2. spectator （　　）　　3. legendary （　　）
4. inquiry （　　）　　5. psychology （　　）　　6. promotion （　　）

　　A. 問い合わせ　　B. 認知の　　C. 見物人
　　D. 昇格　　E. 心理学　　F. 伝説の

Listening Section

Part 1 Photographs

英文を聞き、4つの中から最も適切な描写を選びましょう。

1.
Ⓐ Ⓑ Ⓒ Ⓓ

2.
Ⓐ Ⓑ Ⓒ Ⓓ

Part 2 Question-Response

設問に対する応答として、最も適切なものを選びましょう。

3. Mark your answer on your answer sheet.   Ⓐ Ⓑ Ⓒ
4. Mark your answer on your answer sheet.   Ⓐ Ⓑ Ⓒ
5. Mark your answer on your answer sheet.   Ⓐ Ⓑ Ⓒ

Part 3 Short Conversation

会話文を聞いて、各設問に対する最も適切な答えを4つの選択肢から選びましょう。

6. What are the speakers discussing?
   (A) The schedule of a seminar
   (B) The content of a staff excursion
   (C) The organization of a team-building exercise
   (D) The timing of their next health check

7. What session topics are the speakers considering for the seminar?
   (A) Time management and communication skills
   (B) Mindfulness and stress management techniques
   (C) Leadership and team-building
   (D) Public speaking and presentation skills

8. What will the women do next?
   (A) Finalize the seminar topics
   (B) Confirm the speaker lineup
   (C) Add topics to the agenda
   (D) Promote the seminar to staff

Part 4　Short Talk

説明文を聞いて、各設問に対する最も適切な答えを 4 つの選択肢から選びましょう。

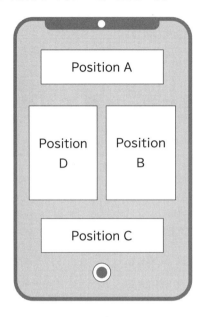

スマートフォンの画面など、TOEIC では日常生活に関するものが多く出ます。

9. What is the speaker offering a trial with?
   (A) A smartphone   (B) A distance learning course
   (C) A program   (D) A diet supplement

10. What most likely did the listener do recently?
    (A) Report a problem   (B) Download an app
    (C) Drop by a gym   (D) Inquire about a fee

11. Look at the graphic. Where will "My Achievement" appear on the screen?
    (A) Position A   (B) Position B
    (C) Position C   (D) Position D

Reading Section

Part 5　Incomplete Sentences

空所に入る最も適切な語句を選びましょう。

12. The new therapy technique is ------- beneficial as the previous one, but with fewer side effects.
    (A) as   (B) more   (C) less   (D) most

13. This medication is considered to be ------- important in managing anxiety symptoms.

    (A) good   (B) better   (C) best   (D) the most

14. The patient's recovery was ------- than expected, thanks to the new rehabilitation program.

    (A) fastest   (B) faster   (C) fast   (D) more fast

15. The study found that cognitive therapy was ------- effective in reducing symptoms of depression.

    (A) much   (B) most   (C) many   (D) more

16. Among all the treatments tested, this one showed the ------- improvement in patient outcomes.

    (A) greater   (B) coldest   (C) more   (D) greatest

Part 6 Text Completion

Part 6 では「広告」もよく出題されるよ。

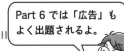

Questions 17-20 refer to the following job advertisement.

Do you have experience as a swimming instructor? Did you major in physiology or psychology at university? Since opening our new aquatic center on Chadwick Street in April, Max Sports is ------- (17) seeking motivated professionals. Given the increasing importance of a scientific approach to developing high-level swimmers, we ------- (18) on training methods that effectively balance physical and mental aspects.

-------(19). For example, the new center has an on-site nursery for instructors with young children. We prefer candidates with at least three years of experience as a swimming instructor. While a degree in physiology or psychology is not required, it is preferred. We offer a competitive salary, along with incentives for outstanding performance.

For further details, please visit our Web site or stop by the aquatic center, ------- (20) features a distinctive roof design that sets it apart from other buildings on Chadwick Street.

HR department, Max Sports

17. (A) enthusiastic (B) enthusiasm
    (C) enthusiastically (D) enthusiast

18. (A) are focusing (B) are being focused
    (C) will be focused (D) would have focused

19. (A) The new facility is surrounded by beautiful nature.
    (B) Some building work will be completed behind schedule.
    (C) We operate based on a policy of renewable energy sources.
    (D) We are committed to providing a comfortable work environment.

20. (A) whose (B) which (C) that (D) whom

Part 7   Single Passage

Questions 21-25 refer to the following article.

HARROGATE (June 30) — Harrogate City Football Club announced yesterday that the Football Association had finally approved its promotion to the first division. Compared to its poor performance in recent years, the team has achieved amazing results this season. What magic made this dramatic change possible?

"One of the major revisions we made after last season is our training method." says, the general manager of the club, Collin Powers. "We conducted a thorough review of our approach from every perspective, and it became clear that our traditional methods were outdated."

The club invited professionals from various fields, such as physiologists, nutritionists and even psychiatrists and asked them to help develop a tailored training program. "I was also invited as Head Coach then." reflects John Edman. "Contrary to those staff members, we coaches didn't change our game strategy much. We knew our players could perform better than last season."

Currently, the club's stadium does not meet the requirements of the upper league, especially in terms of size, and the Association gave the club a 'conditional' approval. However, this will not be a significant matter for the club, because its new "Williams Stadium" will be completed by the end of next month. It is named after Alan Williams, the legendary player for the club in the 1960's. Since the stadium will accommodate over one hundred thousand spectators, the team will be fully eligible for promotion to the first division.

Since the club, local businesses and the city signed the agreement for financing the new stadium in 2020, the construction project made a great step forward. "We fully agreed on the idea then," says the former director of sports for the city, Geoff Ogawa, "I am overwhelmed to be invited as mayor to the opening ceremony, and I can't wait."

21. Who was Mr. Ogawa in 2020?
　　(A) A general manager　　(B) A mayor
　　(C) A city official　　(D) A business owner

22. What is suggested about the current stadium?
　　(A) It was supposed to be completed earlier.
　　(B) It was named after a legendary player.
　　(C) It is conveniently located near the city hall.
　　(D) It houses under one hundred thousand fans.

23. What did Harrogate City Football Club change after last season?
　　(A) Its game strategy　　(B) Its head coach
　　(C) Its financial policies　　(D) Its renovation plan

24. Who will most likely attend the opening ceremony?
　　(A) Collin Powers　　(B) John Edman
　　(C) Alan Williams　　(D) Geoff Ogawa

どの人物の名前も文章中に出てくるけれども、惑わされないようにしよう。

25. What is NOT mentioned about Harrogate City Football Club?
　　(A) It was financed by local companies.
　　(B) It suffered from a shortage of staff members.
　　(C) It will meet the size requirements for its new stadium.
　　(D) It did not perform well these past few years.

Unit 11
Aeronautics / Transportation

航空学は、飛行機やヘリコプターなど、空を飛ぶ乗り物の設計や運用を学ぶ分野です。輸送は、物や人を移動させることを指し、私たちの日常生活や経済活動に欠かせない技術です。航空と輸送の技術は、グローバルな移動や物流を支える重要な要素です。

コラム⑪　Part 5『短文穴埋め問題』攻略法

▶問題タイプを見極めよう

短文穴埋め問題では、問題タイプを素早く判断することがとても重要です。すべての問題に均等に時間を費やすのではなく、時間を割くべき設問とそうでない設問を見極めましょう。問題を解き始める前に必ず選択肢を確認して、以下の4つの種類を判別しましょう。

品詞識別問題……英文をすべて読まなくても空所の前後と選択肢を見れば解答できます。

語彙問題……同じ品詞が選択肢に4つ並んでいます。問題文を読み、空所以外の内容把握が必要です。

動詞（時制）問題……一つの動詞の変化形が選択肢に並んでいます。文の意味は取らず、前後の語句から「態」を識別し「主語動詞の一致」を考えましょう。

文法問題……接続詞、前置詞の識別、相関語句、代名詞、関係代名詞、関係副詞、比較、最上級などがあります。

選択肢が全部似ている形かどうか、最初に見て確認すると、解きやすいよ。

Key Vocabulary　英語の意味を下記の日本語から選びましょう。

1. turbulence (　　)
2. departure (　　)
3. additional (　　)
4. spectacular (　　)
5. congestion (　　)
6. refund (　　)

A. 混雑　　B. 目を見張るような　　C. 追加の
D. 乱気流　　E. 出発　　F. 払い戻す

Listening Section

Part 1 Photographs

英文を聞き、4つの中から最も適切な描写を選びましょう。

1.

   Ⓐ Ⓑ Ⓒ Ⓓ

2.

   Ⓐ Ⓑ Ⓒ Ⓓ

Part 2 Question-Response

設問に対する応答として、最も適切なものを選びましょう。

3. Mark your answer on your answer sheet.　　Ⓐ Ⓑ Ⓒ
4. Mark your answer on your answer sheet.　　Ⓐ Ⓑ Ⓒ
5. Mark your answer on your answer sheet.　　Ⓐ Ⓑ Ⓒ

Part 3 Short Conversation

図表に関する会話文を聞いて、各設問に対する最も適切な答えを4つの選択肢から選びましょう。

6. From which gate is their flight departing?
   (A) Gate 4
   (B) Gate 9
   (C) Gate 14
   (D) Gate 19

7. Where are they currently located?
   (A) Terminal A
   (B) Terminal B
   (C) Terminal C
   (D) Terminal D

	Restaurant
Gate 16-20	Terminal D
Gate 11-15	Terminal C
Gate 6-10	Terminal B
Gate 1-5	Terminal A
	Deck | Shop

8. What will the speakers do next?
   (A) Visit the souvenir shop
   (B) Check the flight information again
   (C) Walk to Terminal C
   (D) Visit the restaurant in Terminal D

Part 4 Short Talk

説明文を聞いて、各設問に対する最も適切な答えを 4 つの選択肢から選びましょう。

Map around the Venue

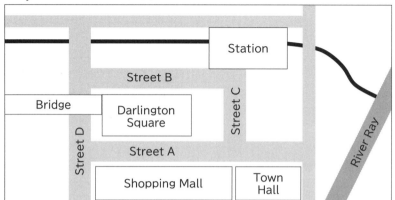

9. Where will be the event held?
   (A) Around the station
   (B) In the plaza
   (C) Under the bridge
   (D) On the streets

10. Look at the graphic. Which most likely is Mansfield Street?
    (A) Street A
    (B) Street B
    (C) Street C
    (D) Street D

11. What are the listeners who will shop at the mall advised to do?
    (A) Use public transportation
    (B) Avoid parking near the stalls
    (C) Present their parking permit
    (D) Walk through the event venue

Reading Section

Part 5 Incomplete Sentences

空所に入る最も適切な語句を選びましょう。

12. The flight was delayed due to ------- weather conditions.
    (A) unexpectedly
    (B) unexpected
    (C) unexpectedness
    (D) expect

13. The airline announced a ------- increase in the number of international flights.
    (A) significantly
    (B) significance
    (C) significant
    (D) signify

14. The captain spoke ------- to reassure the passengers during the turbulence.
    (A) calmly   (B) calm   (C) calmness   (D) calms

15. The new concourse was built to ------- the growing number of travelers.
    (A) accommodation   (B) accommodating
    (C) accommodate   (D) accommodates

16. The airport's ------- has improved dramatically with the recent renovations.
    (A) operate   (B) operational   (C) operator   (D) operation

Part 6 Text Completion

Questions 17-20 refer to the following advertisement

The Holiday Drone Light Show is Coming Back!

The Executive Committee of Ipswich Summer Festival is pleased to inform you that 'the Holiday Drone Light Show' will finally be held again on July 1. -------(17) the show was held at the Cherry Blossoms Festival in April, a large number of positive reviews -------(18) various generations were posted on its social media account. Based on that, the city considered the possibility of reviving it in the future.

Starflyer Co. Ltd., the team of drone show performers, willingly accepted our offer this time too. Apparently, they will use many more drones than the first time and have completely changed the show's contents to be more spectacular. -------(19). What if you could operate a drone with the team members backstage?

Please note that the roads around the venue will be closed from 4 p.m. The city will operate shuttles from Ipswich Station, -------(20) timetable is available on our Web site.
We look forward to your attendance, at 6 p.m., in the Central Park!

17. (A) The first time   (B) Although   (C) Given that   (D) Regarding

18. (A) during   (B) below   (C) under   (D) from

19. (A) However, we regret to inform you that all tickets have been sold.
    (B) Also, there may be a special event before the show.
    (C) A list of sponsors will be unveiled on our Web site soon.
    (D) Your supports for the committee would be appreciated.

20. (A) whose   (B) which   (C) that   (D) whom

Part 6 には文脈に関係なく解ける問題もあるから、あきらめないで！

Part 7 Double Passages

Questions 21-25 refer to the following Web page and notice.

https://example.com

The New Ticket Purchasing App 'Quick Seat' is Now Available!

For greater convenience, Fingland Trains introduced a new ticket purchasing application "Quick Seat" on April 1. It allows customers to purchase tickets far more easily on their smartphones and they will no longer need paper tickets for their journeys. Please see the following instructions and features of our new app:

1. Download the app
Please install "Quick Seat" from this Web site on your smartphone. Payments can be made by credit card, using our previous online system. You can now connect payment apps such as "Easy Pay" or "Fast Pay" to our app for more convenience.

2. Seating Charts
After you input your destination and the number of tickets required, please tap the "seating map" button to view available seats on the train. With the new app, you can choose your preferred seating directly from the train's layout. By tapping the button, the seating chart of the train will appear on the screen. Then, please choose the seats you prefer. Customers can make seat

reservations from 30 days to 30 minutes before their departure unless the train is full. Please note that payment must be made 15 minutes before departure. If it is not made, your reservation will be automatically canceled.

3. Paperless Boarding

With Quick Seat, there's no need for paper tickets. Simply display your digital ticket on your smartphone when the conductor checks your ticket during your journey.

We look forward to traveling with you soon.

Customer Support, Fingland Trains Co., Ltd.

The Problems with Our Online System (updated at 2 p.m., April 22)

We are sorry to inform you that some technical problems occurred with our computer system around 10 a.m. this morning. We have not identified the cause of the problems yet, but your online booking information cannot be displayed on your devices as well as those of our staff at the moment.

Since we are not sure how long it will take for our system to recover, all passengers departing for Sainsbury can take any vacant seat on their express train today. If you booked a first-class seat, we will refund the additional fee later.

We apologize for any inconvenience this may cause you.

Fingland Trains Co., Ltd.

21. What is the main purpose of the Web page?
   (A) To report a technical problem
   (B) To advertise a new appliance
   (C) To announce the latest system
   (D) To promote a special sale

22. What are customers advised to do to use the new system?
    (A) Update their personal information
    (B) Avoid using security software
    (C) Link specific applications together
    (D) Register their bank account details

23. What is suggested about Finland Trains?
    (A) It has stopped operating its old system.
    (B) It encourages its customers to pay online.
    (C) It no longer sells paper tickets.
    (D) It usually operates trains on time.

24. What is implied about the Quick Seat?
    (A) It has increased the number of customers.
    (B) It is available on any type of digital device.
    (C) It allows customers a month to pay after booking.
    (D) It issues a receipt for the total fare amount.

25. What will the passengers NOT do on the train for Sainsbury on April 22?
    (A) Use the onboard sales service
    (B) Present their smartphone
    (C) Find an alternative seat
    (D) Change their schedule

TOEIC L&R で、時間内に設問 200 番すべて解き終えるには、平均「150 語／分」位の読解スピードが必要です。音声にすると、Listening Section の Part 3 や Part 4 でナレーターが話すスピードと同じ位だと考えましょう。

Unit 12
Climatology/Meteorology

気候学は、地球の長期的な天候パターンや変動を研究する学問で、異常気象や気候変動の原因を探ります。
気象学は、日々の天気予報を含む、短期的な大気の状態を研究する学問です。

コラム⑫　Part 6『長文穴埋め問題』攻略法

▶ 2番目の穴埋めパートもスピード重視で

　Part 6は『長文穴埋め問題』と呼ばれ、1つの文書にある4か所の空欄を埋めていきます。Part 5『短文穴埋め問題』が単文であるのとは異なり、Part 6の文書は複数のセンテンスで構成されています。よって、大半の設問では、空欄のある文だけでなく、その前後の文も読んで解くことが求められます。

　しかし「長文」とは言っても、文書はたいてい1、2段落のみ（計80～120語程度）ですので、**一文書のトピックはほぼ1つだけ**。「設問を解くスピード」に加えて「文書を読むスピード」も速くすることを意識すれば、**Part 6の学習はPart 7へのよい準備**となるでしょう。

まずは文書をすべて読み、文脈を捉えてから解く方が速いよ！

Key Vocabulary　英語の意味を下記の日本語から選びましょう。

1. negotiate （　　）　2. cloudy （　　）　3. comfortable （　　）
4. climatologist （　　）　5. exaggeration （　　）　6. windy （　　）

A. 強風の　　　B. 気候学者　　C. 交渉する
D. 曇りの　　　E. 誇張　　　　F. 快適な

Listening Section

Part 1 Photographs

英文を聞き、4つの中から最も適切な描写を選びましょう。

1.

   Ⓐ Ⓑ Ⓒ Ⓓ

2.

   Ⓐ Ⓑ Ⓒ Ⓓ

Part 2 Question-Response

設問に対する応答として、最も適切なものを選びましょう。

3. Mark your answer on your answer sheet.   Ⓐ Ⓑ Ⓒ
4. Mark your answer on your answer sheet.   Ⓐ Ⓑ Ⓒ
5. Mark your answer on your answer sheet.   Ⓐ Ⓑ Ⓒ

Part 3 Short Conversation

会話文を聞いて、各設問に対する最も適切な答えを4つの選択肢から選びましょう。

6. What type of company do the speakers work for?
   (A) A beverage company
   (B) A weather forecasting company
   (C) A construction company
   (D) A cleaning management company

7. What is the weather forecast for Saturday?
   (A) Rainy and cold   (B) Hot and sunny
   (C) Cool and cloudy   (D) Hot and windy

8. What will the woman do next?
   (A) Check the number of cans again
   (B) Confirm the event schedule
   (C) Ensure that everyone is prepared for the windy conditions
   (D) Inform the customers about the new product

Part 4 Short Talk

説明文を聞いて、各設問に対する最も適切な答えを4つの選択肢から選びましょう。

9. When will the event finish?
   (A) On December 15   (B) On December 16
   (C) On December 17   (D) On December 18

10. Who is Harrison McCarthy?
    (A) A historian   (B) A printer   (C) A professor   (D) An artist

11. According to the speaker, what will Jimmy Wilson most likely do?
    (A) Promote the permanent exhibition
    (B) Talk with Amy Hammond
    (C) Introduce his latest art studies
    (D) Explain the history of the museum

Reading Section

Part 5 Incomplete Sentences

空所に入る最も適切な語句を選びましょう。

12. The ------- of the weather patterns made it difficult to predict the storm's path.
    (A) variation   (B) vary   (C) various   (D) varying

13. The scientist ------- the importance of collecting accurate climate data.
    (A) emphasizing   (B) emphasized   (C) emphasizes   (D) emphasis

14. Due to ------- weather conditions, the outdoor event was postponed.
    (A) unpredictable   (B) unpredictably
    (C) unpredictability   (D) predicted

15. The meteorological team ------- monitors changes in atmospheric pressure.
    (A) constant   (B) constantly   (C) constancy   (D) constants

16. The report provided a ------- analysis of the long-term effects of global warming.

    (A) detailed   (B) detailing   (C) detail   (D) details

Part 6   Text Completion

Questions 17-20 refer to the following advertisement.

Spend Your Summer Holidays in a Unique Way

Have you decided on your plans for the summer holidays yet? If not, what about spending this summer differently from every other year? Greggs Travel would like to offer you a tour of the tropical Chamorro Islands, ------- (17) you might realize something new.

This tour aims to deepen your understanding of the islands' natural environment. The tour ------- (18) some unique activities, such as a field trip with local climatologists and meteorologists. ------- (19). No need to worry. ------- (20), these experts won't be giving lectures; they will guide you to the mountains and seashores, and even snorkel with you in the sea. Through the tour, you'll gain greater awareness of changes happening in the global environment.

---

17. (A) that   (B) where   (C) whether to   (D) those of

18. (A) is included   (B) includes   (C) have included   (D) including

19. (A) Has the number of visitors been increasing?
    (B) Are you sure you have received the itinerary?
    (C) Do they have enough teaching experience?
    (D) Do you think that sounds boring?

20. (A) Unfortunately   (B) Completely
    (C) Basically   (D) Unwillingly

Part 7 Single Passage

Questions 21-25 refer to the following Web page.

https://example.com

Why don't you help us liven up the Little's Festival?

To honor the significant contributions to the development of the town by Wigan Meteorological Observatory, an annual commemorative festival will be held on July 9. - [1] -. The Executive Committee is seeking 20 enthusiastic volunteers for the festival.

The town of Wigan is well-known for its high-quality wheat. The town was originally blessed with rich soils that were ideal for growing wheat. - [2] -. However, the farmers were frustrated by seasonal storms. Since Simon Little, a local meteorologist, built a small weather station in the outskirts of the town in 1925, his surprisingly accurate weather forecasts have consistently amazed the farmers. - [3] -. Perhaps they could not thank him enough for his invaluable information. Even now, it is not an exaggeration to say that we rely on his contributions. That is why the festival was renamed "Little's Festival" in 1985.

Since the first festival was held here in 1970, a countless number of local people have been devoted to supporting the festival as staff members in various ways. Some have advertised our events in the media and negotiated for permission to use the town's convention hall with town officials. Others have asked renowned TV weather forecasters to open seminars, and have even operated shuttles between the venue and the station on the day of the event. - [4] -.

Staff members will be paid, receive free meals and be offered refreshments during the festival. You can now apply for positions on our Web site no later than June 5. Please make sure to upload a copy of your recent photo ID for your application. Short-listed candidates will be contacted by e-mail regarding an interview by June 14.

21. What is the purpose of the Web page?
    (A) To revitalize agriculture
    (B) To recruit staff for an event
    (C) To honor the local farmers
    (D) To promote a seminar

22. The word "renowned" in paragraph 3, line 5, is closest in meaning to
    (A) freelanced   (B) recognized   (C) experienced   (D) awarded

23. What did the previous staff NOT do?
    (A) Host a seminar
    (B) Provide transportation services
    (C) Advertise the festival
    (D) Meet with the town officials

24. In which of the positions marked [1], [2], [3], and [4] does the following sentence best belong?
    "Obviously, weather forecasting plays a crucial role in agriculture."
    (A) [1]   (B) [2]   (C) [3]   (D) [4]

25. What is suggested about the Little's Festival?
    (A) It was sponsored by some local businesses.
    (B) It was initiated by local farmers.
    (C) It was held in another name in 1980.
    (D) It was supported by town officials.

Unit 13
Employment/ Job Hunting

就職活動では、Employment（雇用）と Job Hunting（就職活動）が重要なテーマです。企業の求めるスキルを知り、自分に合った職場を探すための英語力が求められます。履歴書や面接での表現を練習することで、国際的な職場にも対応できる力がつくでしょう。

コラム⑬　Part 7『読解問題』攻略法

▶設問のタイプを意識する

Part7 の設問には、下記のようなタイプがあります。この「設問のタイプ」を意識して解く練習をしていくと、一見多様に見える各設問のイメージが次第にはっきりとしてきます。そして、「文書のヒントが見つかりやすい場所は」「選択肢ではどのように言い換えられているか」「時間が足りなくなりそうな場合、どの問題は避けた方がよいのか」など、新たな視点が生まれるでしょう。

Part 7 では「**文書を読む力**」と「**設問を解く（選択肢を選ぶ）力**」の両方が要求されます。2 つの力をバランスよく鍛えていきたいものです。

1. 文書の目的・概要を問うタイプ
2. 文書の詳細情報を問うタイプ
3. 選択肢を文書と照らし合わせるタイプ
4. あてはまらない選択肢を選ぶタイプ
5. 書き手の意図を推測するタイプ
6. 単語の意味を問うタイプ
7. 文が入る位置を問うタイプ

Key Vocabulary　英語の意味を下記の日本語から選びましょう。

1. certificate (　　)
2. instrumental (　　)
3. regulation (　　)
4. dedication (　　)
5. comprehensive (　　)
6. application (　　)

A. 包括的な	B. 証明書	C. 献身
D. 申込書類	E. 規則	F. 役立つ

Listening Section

Part 1　Photographs

英文を聞き、4つの中から最も適切な描写を選びましょう。

1.
Ⓐ Ⓑ Ⓒ Ⓓ

2.
Ⓐ Ⓑ Ⓒ Ⓓ

Part 2　Question-Response

設問に対する応答として、最も適切なものを選びましょう。

3. Mark your answer on your answer sheet.　　Ⓐ Ⓑ Ⓒ
4. Mark your answer on your answer sheet.　　Ⓐ Ⓑ Ⓒ
5. Mark your answer on your answer sheet.　　Ⓐ Ⓑ Ⓒ

Part 3　Short Conversation

会話文を聞いて、各設問に対する最も適切な答えを4つの選択肢から選びましょう。

6. What is the woman doing to prepare for the job application?
   (A) Writing her cover letter
   (B) Practicing for an interview
   (C) Reviewing the job description
   (D) Updating her resume

   （設問を読んだだけで、女性が仕事を探していることがわかるね。）

7. What is the man focusing on in his cover letter?
   (A) His teamwork skills
   (B) His experience with specific software
   (C) His communication skills
   (D) His educational background

8. What do the speakers agree on?
   (A) To submit their applications before the deadline
   (B) To attend the company meeting
   (C) To help each other with their current projects
   (D) To prepare for a team presentation

Part 4 Short Talk 🎧53

説明文を聞いて、各設問に対する最も適切な答えを 4 つの選択肢から選びましょう。

9. Who most likely are the listeners?

    (A) Sales managers
    (B) Marketing analysts
    (C) Appliance business owners
    (D) Human resources officers

10. What did the management decide to do yesterday?

    (A) To withdraw from the area
    (B) To merge with another company
    (C) To launch a new product
    (D) To open some shops

11. What are the listeners asked to do?

    (A) Apply for the positions
    (B) Share the information online
    (C) Check the job advertisement
    (D) Submit a list of references

Reading Section

Part 5 Incomplete Sentences

空所に入る最も適切な語句を選びましょう。

12. The company is looking for a candidate with ------- experience in project management.

    (A) broad   (B) narrow   (C) deep   (D) limited

13. During the interview, applicants were asked to describe their ------- in the field.

    (A) knowledge   (B) knowing   (C) knowledgeable   (D) knows

14. The new employee was ------- to adapt quickly to the company's culture.

    (A) willing   (B) reluctance   (C) willingfully   (D) willingness

15. The recruiter was impressed by the candidate's ability to ------- under pressure.

    (A) thrive   (B) survive   (C) strive   (D) arrive

16. The job offer includes a ------- salary and a comprehensive benefits package.

    (A) competitive
    (B) competing
    (C) compete
    (D) competitiveness

単語の形が似ていても、全く違う意味であることも多いから、早とちりしないようにね。

Part 6 Text Completion

Questions 17-20 refer to the following job information.

Cheadle Finance Corporation is seeking a qualified candidate for the position of Senior Analyst at its new branch office. ------- (17) the current situation of the drastically changing finance industry, we will be opening a new office in Hampstead Square. Applicants are required to have a degree in either finance, at least three years of ------- (18) experience and fluency in either Chinese or French language, as well as English. ------- (19).

If you would like to apply for the position, please send your résumé, two letters of reference and certificates ------- (20) your computer and language skills to the human resources department at the following e-mail address: hrdpt@chadlefinace.co.uk no later than 30 November. Successful candidates will be contacted by phone so that we can schedule an online interview.

17. (A) It being faced   (B) Faced   (C) Having faced   (D) Facing

18. (A) manager   (B) managerial   (C) manageable   (D) manage

19. (A) The board of directors will enforce a new company policy.
    (B) The details of the employee benefits will be changed soon.
    (C) Moreover, your travel expenses will be covered by the company.
    (D) Also, expertise in Artificial Intelligence is preferred.

20. (A) demonstrating   (B) demonstrated
    (C) demonstration   (D) demonstrates

Triple Passages

Questions 21-25 refer to the following e-mails and contract.

To:	Roy Shultz <roy.shultz@orangetech.com>
From:	Kate Berry <kate.berry@orangetech.com>
Date:	29 August
Subject:	Request for checking
Attachment:	The first draft for the contract

Dear Roy,

Thank you very much for joining us in the human resources department to interview Sierra Young yesterday. Your insights and suggestions from a global business standpoint were instrumental in our decision to hire her. As you pointed out in the discussion after the interview, Ms. Young has not only outstanding management skills but also a clear-cut insight into the future of the IT industry. This is one of the main reasons we decided to offer her the position of director and we believe she is someone who can help the company find its way in the market.

Please find attached our first draft of the written contract of employment for Ms. Young. I would appreciate it if you could check the details and give me some feedback by next Friday. Please note that this is just a rough draft and we will be adding supplements and further details for each of the articles.

Regards,
Kate

Employment Contract

Orange Technologies Co., Ltd. (the "Company") and Sierra Young (the "Employee") hereby enter into the following contract of employment.

[…]

4. Responsibilities and Job Description
   Manage the marketing department, observe the ongoing overseas operations, evaluate research and development efforts by the other departments, and advise the overseas subsidiaries and affiliated companies.

5. Work Hours
Flexible hours, totaling eight hours per day, to be worked between 8:00 a.m. and 7:00 p.m.

6. Holidays
Holidays include Saturdays, Sundays, national holidays, the period from 23 December to 26 December, and summer holidays (seven days during the months of July and August).

7. Overtime Work
Applicable

[…]

To:	Kate Berry <kate.berry@orangetech.com>
From:	Roy Shultz <roy.shultz@orangetech.com>
Date:	30 August
Subject:	Re: Request for review

Dear Kate,

Hello. I am writing to you to give you my suggestions as follows:

1) Ms. Young will have to attend the monthly online meeting of the board of directors as an advisor. I would suggest including it in her responsibilities.

2) Since our rules and regulations were revised last month, we have to be careful about her overtime hours.

3) Meanwhile, we have already been working remotely a few days a week for the past two years. I think this should also be reflected when we write a new contract. It may be time for us to reconsider the terms of our working hours. Why don't we ask our legal department for their opinion?

I'll also be happy to check the supplemental documents if necessary.

Regards,
Roy

21. Which department does Mr. Shultz most likely work in?

    (A) International

    (B) Legal

    (C) Human Resources

    (D) Public Relations

22. In the second e-mail, which article does Mr. Shultz NOT mention?

    (A) Article 4

    (B) Article 5

    (C) Article 6

    (D) Article 7

23. What will probably happen to the attachment soon?

    (A) It will be forwarded to the marketing department.

    (B) It will be included in the minutes.

    (C) Some revisions will be made to it.

    (D) The Employee will make comments on it.

24. What will Ms. Berry most likely do next?

    (A) E-mail Mr. Shultz her drafts for additional documents

    (B) Request the board of directors to interview Ms. Young

    (C) Finalize the draft with her immediate supervisor

    (D) Organize an online meeting with her client

25. What is suggested about the Employee?

    (A) She will be supervising the IT department.

    (B) She will be advising the company executives online.

    (C) She has experience working in other countries.

    (D) She occasionally works at home

Unit 14
Biology/Zoology

Biology（生物学）は、生命の仕組みや進化、生物の相互作用を研究する学問です。Zoology（動物学）は、動物の生態や行動を研究します。生き物のことを理解することで、環境保護や種の保存にも役立つ知識を学びます。

コラム⑭　TOEIC® Listening & Reading Test のスコアの目安は？

▶ TOEFL iBT や IELTS、英検への換算表

TOEIC と TOEFL iBT、IELTS、英検の取得スコアと取得級の目安

TOEIC スコア	TOEFL iBT スコア	IELTS スコア	英検取得級
990 〜 950	120 〜 99	9.0 〜 8.0	1 級
945 〜 730	98 〜 74	7.5 〜 6.0	準 1 級
725 〜 535	73 〜 61	5.5 〜 5.0	2 級
530 〜 430	60 〜 45	4.5 〜 4.0	準 2 級
425 〜 380		3.5 〜	3 級
375 〜 300			4 級
295 〜			5 級

大体の目安を見て、目標を立ててみよう。

Key Vocabulary　英語の意味を下記の日本語から選びましょう。

1. echolocation (　　　)　　2. endangered (　　　)　　3. evaluation (　　　)
4. survey (　　　)　　5. discovery (　　　)　　6. migration (　　　)

A. 発見　　　　　　　　B. 評価　　　　　　C. 移住
D. 絶滅の危機にある　　E. 反響定位　　　　F. 調査

Listening Section

Part 1 Photographs

英文を聞き、4つの中から最も適切な描写を選びましょう。

1.
   Ⓐ Ⓑ Ⓒ Ⓓ

2.
   Ⓐ Ⓑ Ⓒ Ⓓ

Part 2 Question-Response

設問に対する応答として、最も適切なものを選びましょう。

3. Mark your answer on your answer sheet.　Ⓐ Ⓑ Ⓒ
4. Mark your answer on your answer sheet.　Ⓐ Ⓑ Ⓒ
5. Mark your answer on your answer sheet.　Ⓐ Ⓑ Ⓒ

設問が疑問詞の形でない、平叙文の場合でも、会話がナチュラルに流れているものを選ぼう。

Part 3 Short Conversation

図表に関する会話文を聞いて、各設問に対する最も適切な答えを4つの選択肢から選びましょう。

Animal Communication Methods

Species	Communication Method
Dolphins	Echolocation
Bees	Dance Communication
Elephants	Infrasound
Birds	Songs and Calls

6. What are the speakers discussing?
   (A) Their favorite animals　(B) A project on animal communication
   (C) A field trip to the zoo　(D) A biology class final exam

7. According to the chart and the conversation, which animal does the woman want to study?
   (A) Dolphins　(B) Bees　(C) Elephants　(D) Birds

8. What does the man suggest including in the project?

   (A) The history of animal communication

   (B) A comparison of habitat environments

   (C) The migration patterns of animals

   (D) Different animals' communication methods

Part 4　Short Talk

説明文を聞いて、各設問に対する最も適切な答えを4つの選択肢から選びましょう。

9. What most likely happened to Barbeck Nature Village before August 1?

   (A) It held a series of events.

   (B) It partially underwent refurbishment.

   (C) It invited some visitors for free.

   (D) It periodically updated its Web site.

10. What is the business offering until August 21?

    (A) Free admission to the events

    (B) Commemorative gifts

    (C) Reduced accommodation fees

    (D) Discount vouchers

Part 4の3問中、最後の問題で「聞き手がすること」に関する問題は、最後だけを聞いてわかることも多いから、あきらめないようにしよう。

11. What are the listeners advised to do to join the events?

    (A) Purchase a ticket beforehand

    (B) Present their membership card

    (C) Input a promotional code

    (D) Reserve a room online

Reading Section

Part 5　Incomplete Sentences

空所に入る最も適切な語句を選びましょう。

12. The study focused on the ------- behavior of certain marine species during the breeding season.

    (A) migratory　　(B) migration　　(C) migrate　　(D) migrating

13. The researcher's findings were published in a ------- scientific journal.

    (A) peer-reviewed   (B) reviewable   (C) peer-review   (D) reviewed

14. The conservation efforts aim to ------- the population of endangered species.

    (A) stabilize   (B) stability   (C) stable   (D) stabilization

15. The ------- of the DNA sample was critical for the success of the experiment.

    (A) purity   (B) pure   (C) purify   (D) purer

16. The scientist presented a ------- argument supporting the theory of evolution.

    (A) convincing   (B) convince   (C) convinced   (D) convincingly

Part 6 Text Completion

Questions 17-20 refer to the following letter.

Hawkridge Pet Store
24 Upper Brook Street, Hawkridge
Portsmouth, PO1 1JN

22 February

Dear valued customers,

You may have heard that the city ------- (17) a total ban on releasing designated foreign species in the Portsmouth Area last month. This mainly aims to ------- (18) the original ecosystem around the city.

------- (19). As long as you are only keeping them as pets, you will not have any problems. We have already set up a consultation desk in each of our stores, so you can ask any questions you may have about the new regulations.

Since we fully agree on the city's initiative, we have also renewed our policy. ------- (20), we have stopped selling many of the invasive species. Additionally, to purchase any foreign species, customers are required to submit a photocopy of their ID card.

We would appreciate your understanding of our new policy.

Jonathan Andrew
Manager, Hawkridge Pet Store

17. (A) implemented (B) was implemented
    (C) would implement (D) had been implementing

18. (A) preserve (B) preservative (C) preservation (D) preserving

19. (A) However, pet stores are exempted from these new rules.
    (B) Accordingly, we decided to relocate our main store.
    (C) The new regulation also prohibits us from feeding them.
    (D) This does not mean a complete ban on owning foreign species.

20. (A) Seemingly (B) Alternatively
    (C) For example (D) If necessary

Part 7 Single Passage

Questions 21-25 refer to the following e-mail.

To:	Douglas Wells <d.wells@best-line.net>
From:	Grace Warden <g.warden@islingtonzoo.org>
Date:	July 7
Subject:	Summer events in 2025

Dear Mr. Wells,

Thank you for your continued patronage. For our 50th anniversary, we will be offering our valued visitors a series of special events from August 13 to 15. We would appreciate it if you could spare a few minutes to answer our online customer survey about the events. - [1] -.

Based on our visitors' answers, we will finalize the details of the event content and time schedules. - [2] -. If you participate in the survey, you may be invited to one of the events. Our tentative plans are as follows:

August 13: Night Jungle Tour
Have you ever seen the wildlife at night? The tour starts at 9 p.m. and lasts an hour. Due to the limited number of special vehicles, we are inviting up to 20 people to join. For safety reasons, children unattended by their guardian are not allowed to join the tour. Let's explore the thrilling night jungle!

August 14: Let's feed your favorite animals!
What and how do your favorite animals eat? Although feeding the animals is normally prohibited in the zoo, only 15 people can feed their favorite animals with zoo keepers after the zoo closes at 5 p.m. Please note that some of the animals will be unavailable because of their sensitive nature.

August 15: Discover the World of Animals
On the final day of our event week, we will invite 50 people to our new theater before its grand opening the following day. - [3] -. The animal world created by our state-of-the-art equipment will allow the audience to experience the life of animals with all five senses.

If you are interested in any of the above, please click the link islingtonzoo/survey/summer/2025, answer the questionnaire and apply for one of the events. Please be sure to comment about your favorite animal at the bottom of the form. We are anticipating a lot of applicants, so there will likely be a ballot for the invitations. - [4] -.

We look forward to hearing your evaluations, suggestions and opinions.

Sincerely,
Grace Warden
Promotion Manager, Islington Zoo

21. What is the main purpose of the e-mail?
    (A) To answer a customer survey
    (B) To invite new visitors to the events
    (C) To advertise the grand opening
    (D) To ask for suggestions

22. What is true about the zoo?
    (A) It has been highly evaluated for years.
    (B) It will open a new theater on August 16.
    (C) It holds some events every summer.
    (D) It will decide the event dates soon.

23. The word "anticipating" in paragraph 6, line 4, is closest in meaning to
    (A) recruiting   (B) promoting   (C) listing   (D) expecting

24. In which of the positions marked [1], [2], [3], and [4] does the following sentence best belong?
    "Winners will be notified by e-mail by August 1 at the latest."
    (A) [1]   (B) [2]   (C) [3]   (D) [4]

25. What is suggested about Douglas Wells?
    (A) He will be attending an event.
    (B) He will be applying for membership.
    (C) He has conducted a survey online.
    (D) He has visited the zoo before.

Review

Listening Section

Part 1 Photographs

英文を聞き、4 つの中から最も適切な描写を選びましょう。

1.
   Ⓐ Ⓑ Ⓒ Ⓓ

2.
   Ⓐ Ⓑ Ⓒ Ⓓ

3.
   Ⓐ Ⓑ Ⓒ Ⓓ

4.
   Ⓐ Ⓑ Ⓒ Ⓓ

Part 2 Question-Response

設問に対する応答として、最も適切なものを選びましょう。

5. Mark your answer on your answer sheet.   Ⓐ Ⓑ Ⓒ
6. Mark your answer on your answer sheet.   Ⓐ Ⓑ Ⓒ
7. Mark your answer on your answer sheet.   Ⓐ Ⓑ Ⓒ

Part 3 Short Conversation

図表に関する会話文を聞いて、各設問に対する最も適切な答えを 4 つの選択肢から選びましょう。

A	👩 👨	B
	Bathroom	

C	D	Elevator

8. What is the speakers' field of expertise?

   (A) Molecular Biology   (B) Mechanical Engineering
   (C) Architecture   (D) Business Management

9. According to the diagram and talk, where will the specimens be located?

   (A) Room A   (B) Room B   (C) Room C   (D) Room D

10. Which room will be the first to have items moved next week?

    (A) Room A   (B) Room B   (C) Room C   (D) Room D

Part 4 Short Talk 🎧61

説明文を聞いて、各設問に対する最も適切な答えを4つの選択肢から選びましょう。

11. Where is the announcement probably being made?

    (A) At a station   (B) At an airport
    (C) On a train   (D) On a plane

12. What are the listeners advised to do at the next stop?

    (A) Change to another train   (B) Check the timetable
    (C) Go to the next platform   (D) Claim a refund

13. How can the listeners receive a meal coupon?

    (A) By giving the staff their ticket
    (B) By purchasing a ticket online
    (C) By visiting any restaurant
    (D) By reviewing the service

Reading Section

Part 5 Incomplete Sentences

空所に入る最も適切な語句を選びましょう。

14. The experiment ------- by the research team to test the hypothesis was successful.

    (A) conducted   (B) conducting   (C) conduct   (D) conducts

15. ------- the laboratory equipment is expensive, it is essential for accurate results.

    (A) Since   (B) Although   (C) Despite   (D) Due to

16. The data analysis revealed a correlation ------- the variables.
    (A) among   (B) between   (C) with   (D) in

17. The research paper was revised ------- it could be published in a prestigious journal.
    (A) so that   (B) despite   (C) because   (D) however

18. The professor suggested ------- more samples to increase the reliability of the study.
    (A) collect   (B) collecting   (C) to collect   (D) collected

19. The study's findings were significant ------- they provided new insights into the field.
    (A) while   (B) because   (C) when   (D) though

Part 6 Text Completion

Questions 20-23 refer to the following notice.

Train Services to be Suspended on Some Lines on January 21

To all passengers:

Due to construction works between Acton Station and Chester Station, Arriva Train Company ------- (20) its train services to Wellington, Doncaster and Fortnum from 9:00 a.m. to 2:00 p.m. on January 21. ------- (21). This will likely delay some passengers, especially those going to Archway Airport as it may take approximately double the time due to the detour.

For passengers going to the airport, we recommend taking our temporary shuttle bus services from the West Terminal, ------- (22) will be operating directly to the airport terminal. The timetable is now available on our Web site. ------- (23), they are advised to take the subway to Bolton Station near the airport.

We apologize for any inconvenience this may cause you.

99

20. (A) will be suspended (B) will have been suspending
    (C) will suspend (D) will have suspended

21. (A) There will be no direct trains in these directions
    (B) The railway construction will last for a few days.
    (C) Some corrections will be made to the new timetable.
    (D) The new terminal station will be opened next month.

22. (A) some of which (B) some of them
    (C) any of which (D) any of them

23. (A) If necessary (B) Accordingly (C) For details (D) Alternatively

Part 7 Triple Passages

Questions 24-28 refer to the following Web pages and e-mail.

---

http://www.machigivillage.or.jp

~ NISHIDA SYUZŌ (Japanese Sake Brewery) ~

The MACHIGI Area, which has been an area blessed with abundant pure water and a moderate climate, is well-known for the production of high-quality rice in this country. These favorable conditions have contributed to the production of Japanese sake in the village. Ever since Shōnosuke Nishida established his first sake brewery in 1862, his family has been producing the finest sakes, such as their signature "MACHIGI NO SAKURA (cherry blossoms in Machigi)".

The brewery has a shop near the station. The shop is open from 10:00 A.M. to 3:00 P.M. on weekdays, and closed on weekends. Visitors to their brewery are all welcome during its business hours, unless it is too busy. Every winter, a special event is held in the brewery offering up to ten visitors a chance to join the sake brewers in the preparation process for the upcoming brewing season. Why not experience the world of traditional Japanese sake for yourself? For further information, please visit the Web site at www.nishidasyuzo.co.jp.

http://www.spiritsworld.com

Over 150 Years of Tradition Living in the Modern Age

NISHIDA SYUZŌ, Machigi Village

"We were touched by their craftsmanship! We've never had such mellow and flavorful sake in our lives. We highly recommend any of their products, especially the 'MACHIGI NO SAKURA', which is also introduced on the Machigi Village Web site. We were so lucky to have a chance to attend the exclusive two-night event, which is now so popular among foreign visitors to Japan. Our experience brewing sake alongside the chief brewer, Kenji Kirishima, was unforgettable. His deep knowledge and unparalleled enthusiasm for sake left a lasting impression on us.

The shop is only 10 minutes' walk from Machigi Station and easy to find. They also operate hourly shuttle services from the station to the brewery and the lodge, as the distance is a bit too far to walk. You may want to check the timetable beforehand."

Sally and Oliver Howell (Birmingham, UK)

To:	Editorial Section <editorial@spodetraval.co.uk>
From:	Sarah Kimura <sarah.kimura@machigi-villlage.or.jp>
Subject:	Request for permission
Date:	April 10

Dear Editorial Section,

Hello. When one of my colleagues was browsing on your Web site 'Spirits World' a few days ago, she happened to find a comment by Mr. and Mrs. Howell. We are very happy to hear that they had a great time at NISHIDA SYUZŌ sake brewery in our village last month.

Since their comments and the photos of them working with Mr. Kirishima on your Web site are very impressive, we would appreciate it if you would kindly allow us to post their positive review and wonderful photos on the village Web site.

If this is possible and there are no copyright concerns, we are wondering if you could contact Mr. and Mrs. Howell to ask for their permission.

We look forward to hearing from you soon.

Kind regards,
Sarah Kimura
International Promotion staff, Machigi Village Office

24. According to the first Web page, what is mentioned about the area?
    (A) It has been promoting a variety of local specialties.
    (B) It is famous for its production of superior grain.
    (C) There are a large number of foreign visitors.
    (D) Its picturesque views are often posted on travel sites.

25. According to the second Web page, what is most likely true about the shop?
    (A) It changes business hours by season.
    (B) It is a family-owned business.
    (C) It closes early if the items sell out.
    (D) It is easy to find from the station.

26. On the second Web page, the word "unparalleled" in paragraph 1, line 7, is closest in meaning to?
    (A) exclusive   (B) outstanding   (C) challenging   (D) specialized

27. What is suggested about Mr. and Mrs. Howell?
    (A) They lost their way to the shop.
    (B) They stayed far from the station.
    (C) They visited the village in February.
    (D) They joined the brewery tour.

28. What is implied about Ms. Kimura?
    (A) She did not know Mr. and Mrs. Howell's contact details.
    (B) She regularly researches the brewing industry.
    (C) She has a friend working for the travel agency.
    (D) She has lived in the area for many years.

著者紹介

松本　恵美子　順天堂大学講師
西井　賢太郎　多摩大学グローバルスタディーズ学部専任講師
Sam Little

テキストの音声は、弊社 HP　https://www.eihosha.co.jp/
の「テキスト音声ダウンロード」のバナーからダウンロードできます。
また、下記 QR コードを読み込み、音声ファイルをダウンロードするか、
ストリーミングページにジャンプして音声を聴くことができます。

Basic TOEIC® for Science and Technology
サイエンス・テクノロジーでTOEIC®スコアアップ
2025 年 1 月 31 日　初　版

著　者Ⓒ　松本　恵美子
　　　　　西井　賢太郎
　　　　　Sam Little

発 行 者　佐々木　元

発 行 所　株式会社　英　宝　社
〒101-0032 東京都千代田区岩本町 2-7-7
TEL 03 (5833) 5870　FAX 03 (5833) 5872
https://www.eihosha.co.jp/

ISBN 978-4-269-66075-5　C1082

［製版：高嶋 良枝／表紙：興亜産業株式会社／印刷・製本：日本ハイコム株式会社］

本テキストの一部または全部を、コピー、スキャン、デジタル化等での無断複写・複製は、著作権法上での例外を除き禁じられています。本テキストを代行業者等の第三者に依頼してのスキャンやデジタル化はたとえ個人や家庭内での利用であっても著作権侵害となり、著作権法上一切認められておりません。